THE FALKLANDS SUMMER

THE FALKLANDS SUMMER

John Branfield

LONDON
VICTOR GOLLANCZ LTD
1987

First published in Great Britain 1987
by Victor Gollancz Ltd
14 Henrietta Street, London WC2E 8QJ

British Library Cataloguing in Publication Data
Branfield, John
    The Falklands summer.
    I. Title
    823'.914[J] PZ7

    ISBN 0–575–03927–2

Typeset at The Spartan Press Ltd,
Lymington, Hants
and printed in Great Britain by
St Edmundsbury Press Ltd, Bury St Edmunds, Suffolk

Matthew Walker hadn't finished writing when the exam came to an end. He fetched his bag from his locker, and went outside the school to join the crowd waiting for the buses.

"How did you do, Matt?" asked Conan.

"Terrible," he said. He hadn't even started the last question. His mind was numb, he felt unadjusted to the real world.

Everyone else was staring up at the sky, and he bent his head back to see what they were looking at. High above, there were two aircraft, one coming up behind the other and gradually closing the gap. They looked very small, but their silhouettes were clear. The one behind had swept-back wings.

"It's a Vulcan," said Conan Trembath. "What's the one in front?"

"Hercules."

Someone said it was a Victor.

The sky was blue and cloudless, except for two vapour

trails which crossed each other. They had been made a while ago and had lost their laser sharpness. The planes edged nearer and nearer until they interlocked, like insects mating.

"What are they doing?"

"Refuelling."

"Are they going to the Falklands?"

It was probably a practice, so near to base. But the Vulcan burnt up so much fuel on take-off that it could have already needed refuelling over West Cornwall. It was possible.

"I expect so," said Matthew.

He wanted to believe that it was real, and that the Vulcan had set out to fly halfway around the world without landing, just as they had when they raided the airfield at Port Stanley. He stared until he was giddy, dazzled by the brightness.

It was exactly one week since the surrender of the Argentines at Port Stanley on Monday, the fourteenth of June. For months the twenty-first of June had seemed important to him, the date of his last exam. Now it didn't seem to matter so much.

The bus came in and there was the usual rush to get on board. He pushed to a window seat, and Conan sat next to him. He tried to look out of the window, but he could no longer see the planes performing their intricate manoeuvre.

Gradually, as he sat in the bus on the journey home, it began to dawn on him that he had finished his last exam. He was free. He wouldn't have to go into school again until next September, apart from a day for returning books when all the exams were finished and for signing on in the sixth form — though he was not at all certain that he would be going into the sixth form. The rest of the summer stretched ahead of him. There would be no more revision, he could do what he liked.

He gave Conan a push. "I've finished," he said.

"Lucky you," said Conan, without any enthusiasm. He had two more papers to do that week.

Matthew got off the bus at the end of the lane, while the others went on to the village of Stennack. He stood on the grass verge for a while and looked at the sky. The aircraft had gone, and there was only a trace of the vapour trails. They were so teased out that they looked more like wispy cloud.

He walked down the road through the valley. A helicopter passed overhead on its way to the coast. All the small birds round about scattered in alarm. He pressed himself against the bank, so as not to be seen. Just before it went out of sight over the hillside, he fired an imaginary missile at it. He looked for the flash of flame, listened for the explosion as it crashed in the next valley, but the engine faded away and then grew loud again as the helicopter circled around and came into view. He threw himself into the tall bracken around the stream on the other side of the road, and took cover. He lay low as it passed overhead, disappearing into the south west. He had not been spotted.

The house was locked. He let himself in, but there was no one he could gloat to about the early start to his holidays. He made himself some rounds of toast and peanut butter, and drank some milk out of a bottle in the fridge. Then he went up to his bedroom and threw his haversack of school books into a corner, thinking that they wouldn't be wanted again. He found his swimming trunks and a towel.

From the house there was a footpath through the valley to the beach, and he set off at a jog. About halfway, where the path began to slope steeply down, he turned off into a narrow track that kept to the side of the valley, through heather and gorse. Ahead was an outcrop of rock.

With the moorland and the sea, it was very much Falklands country. He thought it looked like the hills around San Carlos bay. He slipped into the observation post beneath the overhang. Robert James was there, as he had half expected; he had no exams that day. Although it was hot, he wore a dark green storm jacket, and had a pair of binoculars slung around his neck. Various pieces of equipment were on the ground beside him.

"Ho," said Matthew.

"Ho," answered Robert, without taking his eyes off the valley. The three of them always greeted each other in this way, because everyone else said 'Hi'.

He sat down beside him, with his back to the rocks. The gorse and bracken grew to within a few feet of the stone. It was just high enough to screen them, while they could see over the top and command a view of the whole valley. It made a good observation post.

Robert raised the glasses to his eyes and scanned the opposite hillside.

"Anything to report?"

"No."

The slope on the other side was more exposed to the wind and there was no bracken, only heather and moorland grasses. The grass bent in waves as the wind blew across it. There was very little cover except for an old quarry filled with hawthorn in blossom, pink and white. Several paths led to it across the hillside.

Robert lowered his glasses and turned his wrist to glance at his watch. He pressed the button of the cassette recorder at his side and spoke into the microphone.

"Seventeen-oh-five hours. No movement on the hillside."

A click as he switched off.

On their side of the valley the moors stretched to the cliffs. The skyline was uneven with mine burrows, and a steep track went up the side of the hill. It had been bulldozed for the American tanks, training on the moors in preparation for the landings on the Normandy beaches during the Second World War. The whole landscape had been scarred. There were holes dug by the old miners prospecting for tin, others made by the explosion of bombs and landmines, some dug as foxholes by the troops. There was plenty of cover for snipers.

Matthew scanned the hillside, sweeping around until the dark, north-facing side of the valley fell away in a sudden drop. The deep V at the end was filled with the sea, navy blue in colour and flecked with white, an island in the middle. There were no boats in sight. The warships retired beyond the horizon during the day, to come in close to the beaches under the cover of darkness to begin their bombardment of the enemy positions.

He continued turning through one hundred and eighty degrees, scanning now the sunny side of the valley. There was less cover here, up to the point where the two streams joined and where there were a lot of willows, low and scrubby.

A kestrel strayed into the airspace of the valley. It was a total exclusion zone and the swallows saw it off. They flew above it and dived down, buzzing it closely. They escorted it back to the cliffs.

Robert hadn't taken his eyes off the moorland above the low wood. He picked up his microphone and switched on.

"Seventeen-ten hours," he said quietly. "Still no movement on the hillside. This is the latest she's been. I suspect she is lying low in the heather and gorse over the top of the hill."

"Do you think she heard me coming?"

"That wouldn't make any difference."

"What's happening?"

"She's anxious, there's something odd going on." Robert spoke into the microphone again. "The two crows have left the hawthorn and flown up the valley. . . There are no rabbits left in the field by the stream, they've all gone to ground one by one. . . Everything on the slope is very still."

He switched off. "Listen," he said.

Matthew listened. There was the roar of the waves breaking on the beach. Some days it came from the cove at the end of the valley, some days from over the hill. It was always in the background, but you only realised it was there when it stopped, on the rare occasions when the sea was calm.

There was the rustle of the wind in the grasses. One of Mr Vellanoweth's cows lowed in the next valley. A dog barked, a long way away.

Suddenly there was a sound like distant machine-gun fire. Matthew looked across at Robert.

"The stonechats are making a lot of noise," he said. "They sound very agitated." Three or four of them flitted down the valley, from gorse bush to gorse bush.

Robert switched on the recorder. "Seventeen-twelve hours," he murmured, with a rapid glance at his watch. "Something in the next valley. I can see a movement through the gorse on the edge of the slope."

Matthew was momentarily annoyed that Robert always saw everything first. No matter how hard he tried, staring until his eyes smarted, his friend always beat him by a fraction of a second.

"There are people coming down through the field. I can see a head, two heads, the figures coming into view now. Two men, one about fifty and the other in his thirties. The younger one dressed in a dark suit, the older one in a brown suit with large checks."

The younger man had a clipboard and various papers, and they came into the field in the lower part of the valley, right beneath the hide or lookout.

"That's it, we might as well pack up," said Robert, beginning to move. "She'll lie low now until after dark. She might give it a miss altogether."

"Wait," said Matthew.

The men went to the centre of the field, referring to their maps and papers, looking around them and pointing. Then they moved off towards the stream.

At that moment a fox put its head over the brow of the hill. Matthew could see it distinctly, its ears pricked up, very much on the alert.

"Look!" he said aloud, and immediately regretted having made so much noise.

Robert switched on his recorder. "Seventeen-fifteen hours," he intoned. "A fox appears on the ridge, it's the vixen with the white tip to her brush. She has seen the men and is moving very fast, her body low to the ground. . . She reaches the leat and disappears from view. She's in the old water channel, I can see the bracken waving as she passes along. . . She emerges again and makes her way to the quarry. . . She's taken cover there."

The two men, unaware of all the eyes upon them, walked down the side of the stream to the wood. It was in an old rabbit burrow in the wood that White-tip had hidden her cubs, coming every afternoon soon after four o'clock to feed them.

The men were plunging noisily through the trees and undergrowth. There seemed little chance that the fox would come out of her cover after this invasion of the cubs' hideaway, and after waiting a while the two boys packed up and left.

They went back to the footpath. They kept out of sight of the men, one of whom was now pacing along the side of the wood as though he was measuring it. Robert was laden with binoculars and tape recorder, and had a camera slung around his neck. He was walking in front, when he suddenly stopped.

"Can you smell that?" he asked, wrinkling his nose.

Matthew sniffed. There was a strong stench.

"Fox," said Robert.

He hunted around and soon found the droppings. He took a stick and poked them about. They contained bits of fur and lots of beetle shards, quite undigested. The stink was worse than ever.

"Mice and beetles, that's all," he said.

He went on prodding the grey slime, his camera and binoculars bumping together in front of him.

"Aren't you taking it home?" asked Matthew. It was

the sort of thing he would do, in his handkerchief.

"Better not," he said. "But I'd like to get hold of some dead foxes and dissect their stomachs. I'm sure you wouldn't find any evidence of ducks and chickens, just small mammals and insects."

"Are you coming to the beach?" asked Matthew, getting impatient.

"No."

"Why not?"

"I haven't got my trunks," he said. "And anyway, I ought to revise. I haven't finished my exams yet."

They went on to where the paths from the two valleys joined in the wood. Robert went up the other valley to his home and Matthew carried on down to the sea. The character of the valley changed. It was open to the sea winds and the salt air, and there were no more trees. The heather and gorse grew close to the ground, clipped by the wind, and the path was stony underfoot.

When he turned the last corner and the beach opened out before him, he saw that the red flag was flying. A red flag meant that they were loading explosives. Or, more likely, that the lifeguards wouldn't let anyone go into the sea.

It wasn't surprising, as the wind was strong and had built up a heavy swell. The waves seemed to stand one on top of the other, filling the end of the valley. The wind whipped off the crests and the red flag was stretched taut at the top of its mast.

It was a shame. He had hoped that a swim in the waves would have washed away all thoughts of the exams. It would have been a sort of celebration.

There were very few cars in the car park and hardly any people. It was still too early in the season for there to be many holidaymakers, although the lifeguards' hut was already in position and the lifeguards on duty. They were inside the hut and there was no one on the beach.

He could wait until six o'clock — eighteen hundred hours, he mentally corrected himself — and the guards would go. There would be no one to stop him having a swim. But the sea was very rough and it would be stupid to go into it on his own. He turned and walked back up the valley, looking for anti-personnel mines that might have been planted in the path.

His mum was in the house when he got back. "Where have you been?" she asked. "What have you been doing?"

"Down beach," he said.

"Damage?" she exclaimed, with alarm in her voice. She seemed to believe it. She had been reading the newspapers too much.

"Yeh, vandalised the phone box, pulled out all the wires and smashed the windows," he said. "It was great fun."

She looked puzzled. "What did you really say?" she asked.

"Down . . . beach," he repeated slowly.

"Oh," she said. "I wish you'd speak more clearly, you're getting really slovenly. *Downbeach*." She repeated it gruffly, slurring the words together. "How can anyone make out what that means?"

"You must be going deaf, Mum."

He went up to his room and lay on his bed, feeling pleased that the exams were over. He put a cassette in his Walkman and pulled the earphones over his head. The beat of the music — Joy Division — filled his mind, as though it was being played inside his skull. He closed his eyes.

Gradually he became aware of something other than the music entering his consciousness. He could hear a voice calling in the distance. He opened his eyes and saw his mother's face looking round the door, her mouth opening and closing soundlessly. He took off the earphones.

"Matthew," she was saying, her voice suddenly loud. "I've been calling you for ages. Why do you never come when I call? You could try to be on time for meals."

"I try," he said. "But I fail."

"Then try a bit harder. There's nothing worse than getting a meal ready and no one comes to eat it."

"Sorry."

"And take your feet off the bed."

Nag, nag, nag. It was the title of a song from Cabaret Voltaire. It had never been in the charts, but he liked it a lot.

His dad was already at the table and halfway through his meal. "How did it go today?" he asked.

"I only did four out of five questions."

"Why was that?"

"I didn't have time."

"That doesn't sound very promising, Matt."

"I did one good answer, on the Liberal Government of 1907."

"I couldn't answer that," said his mum. "We didn't do that in History when I was at school."

"It was probably Current Affairs," said Matthew.

"Cheeky."

"Only four questions," said his dad. "That's twenty

15

per cent of the marks lost. You must try to plan, Matt. You must think things through."

"I know."

"What were the other questions?"

"I can't remember," he said. He ate fast, trying to catch up, and they didn't ask him any more. They went on talking about some concern of theirs and he shut them out. He was in a world of his own, still hearing the music in his mind. Joy Division were really very depressing. He made an effort to snap out of it.

"Permission to speak," he asked.

They both looked puzzled. "What is it?"

"There were two men in the field down the valley. Do you know what they were doing?"

"No," they said, waiting for him to tell them.

"No, I don't know, I thought you might. . . They wore suits and one had a clipboard, they looked like officials."

"Perhaps they were from the Ministry of Agriculture, looking for badgers."

"Robert says there aren't any in the valley."

They had heard nothing. Matthew thought the men had looked quite sinister, alien in their town clothes.

He went upstairs to his bedroom after the meal, as he had done every evening for the last few months. It had become a habit. He couldn't realise that there was no longer any need.

His desk was between the bed and the window. On the wall above it was the exam timetable, with each exam struck through with a red felt-tip pen, except for that afternoon's. He picked up the pen and crossed out

History paper two, just for the satisfaction of completing it.

Next to it on the wall was a revision plan. It was much scribbled over in black biro, up to the previous evening. And then after that, nothing.

He gazed at them for a while. They represented hundreds of hours of effort. Now it was over, and perhaps it would all come to nothing. It seemed strange to have no work. He didn't really know what to do. There should have been a party that evening, but all his friends still had examinations to sit.

He tore down the timetables, crumpled them up and threw them in the wastepaper basket. He lay on his bed and switched on the radio for the news. It was all about the possibility of a rail strike. Talks between the unions and British Rail had broken down and a total stoppage was likely from the following Monday. The railway chairman predicted that it could last three months, the general secretary of the union said that a state of war existed between British Rail and the National Union of Railwaymen.

It was very boring and he switched to Radio One. Only a week ago the news had still been dominated by the Falklands War. It was so exciting he had listened to almost every bulletin on radio and television, every news headlines.

He had hardly heard of the Falkland Islands before the military government of Argentina claimed and seized them. He knew they had their own postage stamps and it was where Brunel's ship the *Great Britain* had been beached for many years, before it was towed back to Bristol. He thought they were somewhere down towards the Antarctic, about halfway between South America and

Africa. When he saw a map on television at the beginning of the conflict he was surprised how close they were to the mainland. For a moment he couldn't help feeling that they belonged naturally to Argentina.

But then he realised that the people who lived there were British. Their whole way of life was British and they wanted to stay that way. They didn't want to become Argentine, to speak Spanish instead of English, to use pesetas instead of pence. Why should they be made to change?

The Task Force was despatched to recapture the islands. The very name *Task Force* stirred him deeply. It made it sound like a band of tough, highly-trained men setting out on a mission. He longed to be one of them. There was a boy at school who had been only one form above him, who had left to join the paratroopers a year ago and who had sailed with the Force. Matthew had known him, slightly. If only he had been a year older and had his exams out of the way, he could have been there with him.

Instead he had to watch the preparations for war on television. The Task Force left Southampton in the *Queen Elizabeth*, with military bands playing and crowds waving Union Jacks and displaying patriotic banners. The troops lining the decks threw coloured streamers to the people on the quayside and the great ship moved away surrounded by tugs on the water and helicopters in the air.

It was history, he thought. It had always been like this in the past, when a country went to war. And now he was living through it. He felt proud, he wanted to wave and cheer. But most of all he wanted to be one of the heroes sailing away to the South Atlantic.

"They'll never be used," said his father. "It's just a show of force, to strengthen this country's bargaining position."

But Matthew wanted a fight. General Galtieri and his junta had seized a group of islands that didn't belong to them. They were the aggressors, they deserved to be kicked out. He would have liked to see them get a bashing.

He was overjoyed when the Argentine battle cruiser, the *General Belgrano*, was sunk. It wasn't clear whether it was inside or outside the Total Exclusion Zone, or whether it was steaming towards the British Fleet or heading for the mainland. But what did it matter? They had asked for it.

It sank quickly, with a thousand sailors on board. A British hunter-killer submarine had proved a match for the Argentine Navy. "GOTCHA!" he rejoiced, while his dad looked glum.

The landings at San Carlos Bay, the fighting-off of the attacks by Super-Etendards of the Argentine Air Force armed with Exocet missiles, the recapture of Goose Green and Port Stanley, it was all intensely thrilling.

And now the news was just about strikes again.

It was no good lying around in his bedroom, feeling flat after the end of his exams. He had to do something. He wandered outside to have a look at his bikes.

Their house had once been a small farm and had a range of outbuildings at the back, cattlesheds and stables built into the hillside. He used one of these as a bicycle workshop. It was fitted with a bench which he hadn't tidied for a year. It was covered with a jumble of brakes, cables and gears. There was a spare frame hanging from a hook, and tyres and inner tubes were suspended from nails in the beams where horse collars and halters once hung. It all needed sorting out.

He lifted his racing bike by the handlebars and spun the front wheel. He had hardly used it for months and it didn't spin as freely as he would have liked. He had built the bike himself around a Holdsworth frame, using good quality parts. He kept an old production model for everyday use.

He needed to strip the lightweight racer right down and rebuild it, thoroughly cleaning all the components. He needed to get into training again. He had given up racing all through his fifth year at school, in order to concentrate on his exam work. He could take up track events again, though everyone who had gone on cycling when he gave it up would probably be way ahead of him.

He released the front wheel and started cleaning it, using an old toothbrush to rub the metal polish into the rim. Then he buffed it with a strip of rag drawn to and fro between the spokes. He worked meticulously, rubbing the cloth into the space between spoke and rim where the see-saw movement didn't reach. It was good to be doing something practical, after weeks of learning. The metal began to shine in the dimly-lit workshop.

He had nearly finished the wheel when his mother called him from the back door, to say that they were having coffee. He joined his parents in the kitchen.

"It's a shame you only did part of the History paper," said his dad, renewing the subject of exams.

Matthew groaned inwardly. He thought the matter had been dropped, he didn't want any more post-mortems.

"I was hoping the History would pull you up a bit, after what you did in the other subjects."

He knew what his father was referring to. He had not forgiven him yet for what he had done in Art. They had been given the theme at the beginning of term, on the very day when the recapture of the island of South Georgia was announced. "Rejoice, rejoice!" exclaimed Mrs Thatcher on television, interviewed outside Number Ten, Downing Street. He had begun his preparatory work at once.

"What's this?" asked his dad, looking at his sketches of a damaged submarine in a harbour, a helicopter overhead and snowy hills in the background.

"The recapture of South Georgia," said Matthew, quite pleased with the way it was going.

"But what was the subject?"

"A summer's day." His heart sank as he suddenly saw it through his father's eyes. Until then it had seemed quite appropriate.

"What on earth has that got to do with summer?" asked his dad.

"It's summer in this country," said Matthew defensively. "And when it's summer in England, it's winter in the Falklands." He grew more confident. "Argentina invaded as winter was approaching, so that any counter-attack would have to contend with the weather." That was why the Task Force had to get there at full speed, before the seas were too rough.

"You've even put snow in it, Matt," said his dad incredulously.

"It's what I associate with a summer's day," said Matt. "The recapture of South Georgia." It seemed fair enough to him.

"But they expect sun and heat and colour."

So he had a go at a beach scene, with a blue sea and white sands covered with sunbathers in red costumes. It looked terrible, he was no good at figures. Having tried to satisfy his dad, he went back to his first idea.

His Art teacher wasn't very pleased, either.

"But it's true, it really is what I associate with a summer's day, more than anything else." He had convinced himself by now.

When he mounted his sketches and drawings of submarines and helicopters, his dad rang the Art teacher at school. In the end they allowed him to go ahead with his painting of South Georgia as long as he wrote an explanation and pinned it to his finished work, so that the examiners could make sense of it.

He never told his dad that for his English essay he wrote a very colourful account of how Colonel H. Jones lost his life leading an attack against an Argentine machine gun position at Goose Green. He couldn't remember what the subject was supposed to be.

"There's nothing we can do about it now," said his mum. "We've just got to wait for the results."

Matthew felt that all the excitement of finishing the exams was beginning to fade, and that the results would hang like a cloud over the rest of the holidays.

The next morning he stripped the bike, placing all the pieces on the floor around him. He soaked some of the parts in paraffin, sitting them in old four-litre ice cream tubs. He finished cleaning and polishing the front wheel and started on the back. It was taking the whole day and he wanted to go into the town before the shops closed, so he gave up all thoughts of reassembling the Holdsworth and set off on the production model.

It was five miles into the local town. The bike was heavy and slow, but it was still pleasant to be cycling along, up and down hills in the fresh air. As he entered the town he passed the school. He thought of all the poor kids still inside, Robert and Conan in the school hall where the exams were held. It gave him a feeling of pleasure and renewed his sense of freedom.

He made for the cycle shop and bought handlebar tape and new cables. Then he went to a government surplus store, full of junk furniture and cheap clothes. He had already picked out what he wanted. He bought a pair of camouflage trousers for six pounds ninety-five and a black beret for thirty-five pence. He strapped the parcel to the carrier of the bike with expanding elastics and rode home.

Back in his bedroom he put on a white tee shirt and the camouflage trousers, short white socks and trainers. He already had an army-style pullover, in khaki wool with material patches on the shoulders and elbows, and he pulled it over his head. He stared at his image in the mirror, hardly recognising himself.

He went down to the evening meal as soon as his mum called him. His dad was already sitting at the table. He looked up as Matthew entered.

"What's that you're wearing?" he asked.

"It's my cami trousers," said Matt casually, as he sat down at his place.

"Cami trousers?" repeated his dad, searching around for the joke he knew was there somewhere. "What are they for — kamikaze missions?"

"I bought them for the holidays."

"I've never heard of cami trousers," said his mum. "I've heard of camiknickers though."

"They're fashionable."

"They look very paramilitary to me," said his dad. "But that's the fashion too, I suppose."

He hadn't seen the black beret yet.

"They're comfortable," said Matt. "And they're very practical, they've got lots of pockets."

The trousers had buttons instead of a zip. "Mum," he asked later, as he helped to wash-up for the first time for weeks (he had been let off helping in the house all through the revision for exams), "the flies keep coming undone. What can I do about it?"

"Make the buttonholes smaller."

"Would you do it for me?"

"You can do it yourself, you've nothing else to do now."

He spent the evening sewing up the buttonholes to reduce the size. It wasn't very neat, but the flies no longer popped open.

He worked at his bike all the next day and had reassembled it by the end of the afternoon. He had taken off the old black handlebar tape and replaced it with gold; the new cables were bright yellow. The bike was sparkling, shining red and gold, as smart as a guardsman. The wheels and pedals spun noiselessly, or with just the faintest hum.

He wanted to take it straight out on the road for a spin. But it was half-past four and he also wanted to know if the vixen had returned to her cubs. Robert would probably be at the hide, after having had an exam the previous day. He decided to ride later.

He jogged down the path from the house. It passed between two hedges of hawthorn, wild plums and elder. The bushes met overhead, forming a leafy tunnel. He swerved between the untrimmed growth; it felt good to be running in uniform.

He came out on the open hillside, with heather above and the tall green fronds of new bracken below. He was just above the level of the tops of the willow trees which filled the bottom of the valley around the stream.

A little further along a stunted sycamore tree grew below the path. There was the end of a rope hanging from a bough, where they used to swing across a depression in the ground. Matthew paused and looked down at it. He had in mind another project for the holidays, and now that he had rebuilt his bike he could make a start on his next scheme.

He lowered himself down the slope, clinging on to the stems of gorse bushes to stop himself from falling. He reached the hollow beneath the tree. This was really the shaft of an old mine that had been capped about a hundred years ago with wood and earth. The wood had rotted and the earth had sunk several feet, without falling right in. It often happened that old shafts in the area opened up without warning. In the village a man in his outside toilet had suddenly felt the earth give way beneath him and he was left sitting on the lavatory pan, suspended by the plumbing over a gaping void.

Matthew eased himself cautiously around the edge of the hollow and climbed over the roots of the sycamore. A few feet away the stream rushed noisily down the valley, tumbling over rocks and stones. He pushed through the undergrowth towards an adit in the hillside, a horizontal entrance to a mine, overgrown with ferns and bracken. It had a stone wall on either side, and an enormous slab of slate as a lintel. He crept inside and waited for his eyes to adjust to the darkness.

It was not quite high enough for him to stand upright. The old miners must have been very small, or had walked with a stoop. It smelt dank, and he could hear water trickling. There were ferns growing in cracks in the walls.

It was dark and cold, but he had always thought, ever since they used to play there, that it would make a good nuclear shelter. The tunnel probably linked with others, a network of passages stretching for miles underground. The entrance was only four minutes from the house. If they could get inside before the Bomb dropped, they would be secure.

They would have to explore the workings. If they knew their way around, they would have the advantage over anyone else who tried to invade them. They would have to build up a supply of stores, so that they could live down there for at least two weeks while the nuclear fall-out was dropping like snow outside. They would need tins of food, candles and matches in waterproof containers, perhaps an oil heater and cans of paraffin because the outside temperature would drop below freezing.

They could build a base camp in the deepest part, with benches and beds, and gradually add to their stores throughout the summer. By the beginning of next term they would have a bunker as secure as any in NATO.

He shivered in the damp and returned to the bright sunlight.

Having hauled himself by the gorse bushes out of the

hollow, he went on to join Robert at the lookout. As he expected, he was in his usual position.

"Ho," he greeted him.

"Ho," answered Robert. "I like your camis."

"Thanks," said Matthew. He sat down next to him with his back to the stone. "Have you seen the vixen yet?"

"She's with them now."

She usually stayed no more than twenty minutes. Matthew didn't have Robert's patience, but he could wait that long. He was anxious to explain his plans, but suddenly lost confidence in putting them across to either of his friends. He had an idea that Robert had recently joined CND. If he hadn't actually joined, he was at least in sympathy with them. Matthew thought that somehow he wouldn't believe in bunkers. And Conan would think it was very childish, like building a den.

"I'm thinking of exploring the adit one day," he said casually.

"Great," said Robert. Matt could tell it didn't mean anything.

"Would you come?"

He hesitated. "There's nothing very interesting down there."

"It would make a good nuclear shelter," Matthew said. "We could get it ready. Just in case."

"It's a waste of time," said Robert.

"There'd be no harm, being prepared."

"Nobody would survive, even in there. You'd freeze to death, you'd die of disease or starvation. You'd just drag it out."

"It's worth trying."

"I'd rather die straight away."

"You're defeatist." He was as bad as his dad. "Even if the Bomb doesn't fall, there are other things that could happen. It wouldn't be a bad idea to have somewhere to hide, a sort of bolt hole."

Robert shook his head.

"We could take torches and ropes, and try to go back further than we've been before." He knew he had failed to persuade him. "Anyway, it would be something to do in the holidays," he added.

"Ssh," went Robert. "Look above the quarry, at about eleven o'clock."

Matt looked across at the opposite hillside. It was a bright and windy day, and the shadows of clouds were chasing across the slope. The two crows were sitting as usual in the hawthorn, swaying with the bush as though they grew out of it. They took no notice at all of the fox trotting along the path just below them. It disappeared into the leat, setting the tall heads of bracken swaying as it moved along.

But Robert had said the vixen was already with her cubs. "Is it the male?" Matthew asked.

"No, the males have nothing to do with the cubs," said Robert. "It's a female."

"How do you know?"

"She's got a thinner face than the male."

They watched the length of the leat, and then with a shaking of the bracken the vixen came out and made down the slope towards the wood. She was clearly a different animal; her tail was grey instead of tipped with white. She used the same path into the trees as the other fox.

"That's very interesting," said Robert.

"Why?"

"She could be an unmated sister to White-tip. If they have no young of their own, they'll often help to bring up their sister's cubs."

They waited. Matt thought of the two animals and their young, moving about under the ground, deep within their den or bolt hole. The wind made waves in the long grasses on the opposite hillside.

"Look, there's a cub," he exclaimed, pleased to see it first. It was about the size of a cat, in the corner of the field by the wood.

"It's been there forty-five seconds now," said Robert.

It ran a few paces and then stopped, sniffing around amongst the grass. Another cub ran out of the wood and came to a sudden halt. A third cub peered out of the bracken.

They were soon joined by the vixens, who both lay down in the sun. White-tip stretched out on her side and snapped at a fly. She snapped at the cubs when they came near her, and snarled at one who was more persistent than the others. She did not want to play, she wanted to be left alone.

The vixens and their cubs stayed within a patch of flattened grass in the corner of the field, while the sunlight slanted up the valley and the shadows of the trees lengthened. When the play area was in shade, they slipped away into the wood.

He was late for the evening meal again, but his parents didn't seem to mind too much when he said that he'd been watching foxes. They lingered on at the table, while he ate rapidly to try and catch up.

"Anyway, I've found out who the men were," said his

mum. She was good at finding out things like that.

"Yeh?" he mumbled, his mouth full.

"Mr Vellanoweth's selling up. They were probably estate agents, the farm's being auctioned next week."

It seemed convincing. Jimmy Vell was the farmer who owned the fields in the bottom of the valley. He was old and had no help and the fields were neglected, which was why the grass was long and the furze and bracken pushed in from the edges. It suited the foxes.

"I didn't know that," said his dad.

"It was advertised in the paper as Goosewartha Manor."

"Everyone calls it Jimmy Vell's."

"They describe it as a coastal farm, with rough grazing and moorland, beach rights and an island."

"Does Gullen go with the farm?" asked Matt.

"That's what it said, only they called it Gull Island."

"They would, wouldn't they?" said his dad. "It's the obvious anglicisation of Gullen."

"I never knew it belonged to anyone, I thought it was just a rock."

"That's all it is," said his dad. "But I hope the National Trust know about the sale. It would be ideal if they could buy the farm."

Matthew pushed his dinner plate aside and started on his pudding, hunched low over the dish and spooning rapidly in one continuous flow. His mum and dad went on talking about Goosewartha, his dad saying that it meant the 'upper wood', as opposed to the lower wood in the bottom of the valley. They had always, as long as Matt could remember, been trying to decide on a Cornish name for their house; it embarrassed them rather that it was called Greenacres.

"We could use Goosewartha in some form as a name for our house," said his dad. "What do you think of it, Matt?"

Matthew was taken by surprise. "Why don't you call it Goose Green?" he said.

They did not appreciate it. They said he was obsessed with war, that it was time he grew up and realised what it really meant. It wasn't all fancy uniforms, said his dad with a glance at his khaki pullover and camouflage trousers. It wasn't all going off to battle with flags flying and crowds cheering. It wasn't all glory. Look at the injured coming back from the Falklands, said his mum. What glory was it for them to be returning home with burnt hands like blackened stumps in plastic bags, or with the skin burnt off their faces? Some of them were so badly deformed that they weren't even going to be allowed to appear in the victory parade.

"All right," said Matthew, keeping his head down. "I know."

Some were blinded, they went on. Some had lost limbs, some had brain injuries. And they were only nineteen or twenty years old. Would glory help them to live the rest of their lives?

"I know," he said. "There's no need to go on."

He went up to his room. He caught sight of his reflection in the mirror, all khaki and camouflage. It didn't mean anything, it was only a game. He didn't think he was obsessed.

He had been once, perhaps, when he was in the top form of the primary school. He had been fascinated by the Second World War. He did project after project about it, filling books with detailed drawings of the uniforms and armaments, the tanks and aircraft used on both sides. Some of them he had done with Robert and Conan; they had both been keen then. All three of them collected anything to do with the war, gasmasks, helmets, shrapnel. They had found the site of a wrecked plane. It had crashed into a marsh and had lain buried for years. The marsh had been drained and the plane was exposed.

They had filled sack after sack with twisted scraps of old metal, instruments and bullets, dragging them home to store in an outbuilding. As far as he knew, they were still there.

It was unfair to say that he only thought of the excitement of war. He had thought about the men who had died in the plane. He found out all he could about them. They were members of the Polish Air Force. Their plane had crashed soon after take-off; it had exploded on impact and burst into flames. They had been burnt to death.

He had not known if their bodies were still in the cockpit. As they went on digging for fragments, he half expected to find a corpse, still strapped into its charred leather harness, preserved by the peat of the marsh. He was terrified that it would happen, but he kept on scraping away amongst the wreckage. He dreamed about it at night.

He was haunted by these three men from the plains of Central Europe, who in the nineteen forties had found themselves one winter on a temporary airstrip on a wild and stormy cliff top in Cornwall. The unfamiliar sea crashed on the rocks hundreds of feet below. They were a thousand miles from home, on the very edge of war-torn Europe. They had never returned.

*

He yomped down to San Carlos beach, having arranged on the phone to meet Conan there. He wore the headset of his Sony Walkman and above the music of the Dead Kennedies he kept hearing crackling messages about approaching enemy aircraft. The helicopters were active overhead, but the troops had stopped loading ammunition on the beach. The red flag was tied down to the flagpole.

The beach was almost deserted, the lifeguards inside their hut. Matthew jumped down the pebbles and scrambled up the rocks to the spot halfway up the cliffs that they had made their own last summer. It commanded a view of the whole beach and it was away from the sand which got into everything, their clothes, their food, their radios. It was high enough for them never to have to move, whatever the state of the tide, and if it rained there was a cave nearby. It was level enough for them to lie on the rock and sunbathe after a swim.

Soon he saw Conan come over the sea wall and down the pebbles. His hair had an orange-pink streak that he had put in it especially for the exams. He was wearing a pink fluffy jumper, torn and patched jeans, and baseball boots. He went straight down the beach to the bar of sand across the cove; it had been swept clean by the receding tide. He moved across it, dragging one foot sideways or scraping with a heel as he hopped backwards to make lettering on the untrodden surface. The letters spelt out BAD BRAINS. When he had finished he climbed up the rocks to join Matthew. They greeted each other.

"I like your safety-pins," said Matt. The splits in Conan's jeans were fastened with them.

Conan sat on the rocks and looked down on the name of the group he had written in the sand. It showed up well.

"How's the aggro?" asked Matthew. "Are you putting the boot in?"

"No," said Conan. Although he dressed like a punk, he would never speak in character, no matter how hard Matthew urged him on. "What's happening here then?"

"Nothing," said Matt. "It's dead quiet, there's no action."

A couple of Super-Etendards zoomed across the entrance to the cove, emerging from behind one headland, passing over the island and disappearing behind the other headland in a few seconds, the noise swelling behind them to a great roar that gradually died away again.

"We might as well have our swim."

They changed into their trunks and went down to the water's edge. Matthew stepped into the sea; it was freezing cold. He steeled himself and walked straight out into the waves which broke against his knees, his thighs. He waded faster and the next wave splashed over his stomach. The water resisted his progress as he pushed his legs through it. A few small waves and then he saw a breaker approaching. He poised himself and dived into it just before it broke over him. He came out on the other side and swam vigorously towards the open sea. He felt much warmer now.

He turned and looked back, rising on the swell of a wave, and beyond the troughs and crests he could see Conan still standing in the shallows, splashing water over the tops of his legs and arms.

"Come on," he yelled. Conan ran through a haze of spray and plunged.

They kept diving through the waves, the water tearing at their trunks and buffeting their bodies. Matthew felt all his concern over the exams, whether he had done the right questions, whether he had interpreted them correctly, whether he had done well enough to pass, being stripped from him. He felt purified by the waves.

They swam out beyond the breakers, to test the reaction of the lifeguard. He came out of his hut and walked down the beach. He moved his two red and yellow marker flags in the sand, bringing them closer to the receding tide. He stood and watched them.

After a while he blew his whistle. They pretended not to have heard him and continued out to sea towards the distant island. He gave three sharp blasts, so they turned back to the beach.

The three blasts were the signal, revealing that it was safe for them to come ashore. They had left the submarine through the escape hatch and were now making for the land in their wetsuits, each towing behind him his clothes and weapons in a waterproof sack. Matthew swam low in the water, his eyes just breaking the surface, leaving as little wake or disturbance as possible. He watched the shoreline cautiously, in case the signal was a trick. There was no one in sight, only the secret agent on the sand. They moved within the headlands of the cove, which closed around them.

He touched bottom and waded ashore, his pack still floating behind him. He made straight for their contact.

"Don't go out beyond your depth," the man said.

It was the password.

"We know the beach," said Matthew, in the coded reply.

Everything was going according to plan and they ran along the shore. As he passed over the sand bar he went wild, kicking the sand into the air with his bare feet and scuffing up Conan's giant lettering. Conan tried to push him away, complaining loudly, but he obliterated the words. He didn't like Conan's taste in music.

He rode into town and padlocked his red and gold bike to a lamp-post; it was too valuable to take any risks. The Army Recruiting Office was an ordinary house with a front door and two large bay windows on either side, filled with displays and posters. Beyond the picture of a tank he could see a man in khaki moving around the room.

He went up to the door and into the hallway. Two boys he knew from school were coming out, holding leaflets in their hands. They stopped to talk.

"Are you joining up?" asked Matthew.

"We've thought about it," said one of them. "Are you?"

"I thought I might, I'm not very keen on going into the sixth form."

They weren't keen on the sixth form either.

"Especially if I have to retake my O levels," said Matt. "It seems likely."

"The trouble is, they want O levels here."

"What, in the Army?"

"That's what they say. They can pick and choose, so many people want to join up."

"Oh no," said Matthew. He had thought however badly he had done in his exams he would have no problem joining the Army.

He went into the room on the right. He suddenly felt foolish in his semi-uniform, as though he thought he was already in the Army, and he wished he had worn something different. A sergeant behind a desk was wearing the same sort of khaki pullover with cloth patches, except for the white stripes on the sleeve. Matthew went up to him.

"I want to enquire about joining the Army," he said.

"We've run out of leaflets," said the sergeant. "There's been such a rush on them."

"What should I do?" asked Matt.

"Hang on, I'll see if I can find some more." He rummaged through the drawers in his desk. "You can have these two. But we've been inundated with enquiries, absolutely inundated."

Matthew took the brochures. As he left the building, he was dismayed to see Conan riding by on his bike.

The red flag was flying, straining on its mast. They stood on the sea wall and watched the waves, tier upon tier, crash on to the beach. They felt the salt spray on their lips.

"You could swim in that," said Matthew. It would be fun, diving beneath each breaker, sliding around in the troughs or bobbing about like a cork, being battered by the waves. He wouldn't mind going out in it. He appealed to the guard on duty.

"You'd be mad," he said. "The undertow would suck you down, it would take you right out to sea."

Matt didn't believe him. The lifeguards based their decision on the weakest swimmers, but there was no one else on the beach.

"You wouldn't get me going into that sea," said the guard. "Not without a line."

"If I signed something, to say I didn't want to be rescued," he persisted.

"No way," said the guard.

So they stood and watched the crashing waves and the foam. Far out on the ridge of the furthest wave a mine broke the crest for a moment and then disappeared from sight below the next breaker. Matthew imagined it being driven on to the rocks and exploding on impact. The jagged flash filled the cove, like an explosion in a strip cartoon.

A moment later it bobbed into view again. It really looked like a mine. "What's that?" he asked, pointing it out to Conan.

But it had sunk beneath a crest and for a minute or two there was nothing to see.

"Perhaps it was a seal," suggested Conan.

"No, it was solid and round," said Matt. "And it had a projection on it."

"It sounds like Bill Bailey," said Conan, mentioning their fifth-year tutor at school.

They waited, and then it came up within the curl of a wave and rolled and tumbled further in towards the shore. It was not the shape of a conventional mine, more like a barrel. It was silver in colour.

It remained now almost continuously in sight. They picked up some pebbles and moved across the rocks along the side of the cove to get as near to it as possible. The spent waves rushed and swirled below their feet.

They threw a few pebbles at it. Matthew imagined a direct hit and the huge, irregular star of an explosion flowered again in his mind. But their shots dropped into the sea with a splash, falling short by several metres.

"It's a beer barrel," said Conan.

They watched its slow progress into the cove. They scrambled back along the rocks for more pebbles, and kept throwing at it as it got closer and closer. At last Matthew scored: there was a most satisfying 'clonk', the barrel dipped in the water and righted again.

After that they kept up a continual bombardment, battering the metal drum and trying to drive it closer to the beach.

"Let's try and get it," said Matt.

They went down to the water's edge. From here it looked further out than it had from above. Conan ran down with a receding wave but was a long way from it. The next wave drove him back.

They waited, keeping watch on it all the time. It didn't seem to get any closer. If anything, it seemed to be getting further away.

"We'll make a dash for it," said Matthew. "We'll go in and snatch it."

They waited for the next extra-large breaker, and then followed it back, rushing through the succeeding waves until they were waist-deep. The barrel was sliding back into the jaws of another huge breaker. They grabbed it and hung on, while the wave broke over them, knocking them off their feet and sucking them down and out to sea. They broke surface, gasping for breath, and struggled ashore, still holding on to the barrel.

It floated in the shallow water and they could see lettering on its side. They rolled it over and they read the words IRISH BREWERIES. It grounded on the sand, and they rolled it up the beach. It was half full of liquid sloshing around inside.

"It's still got beer in it," said Conan excitedly. "We could have a party."

They couldn't get it open. They rolled it about, kicking it along the sand. They threw more stones at it. They were wondering whether to drag it up on the cliffs, to roll it down over the rocks and let it splash back into the sea, when the lifeguard came over to them.

"That's aluminium," he said. "It's quite valuable. Any brewery would pay forty pounds for that."

Forty pounds! It was a lot of money. Matthew thought of all the things he could do with his share. It would set him up nicely for the holidays. He could buy a second-hand surfboard. He could go touring on his bike, staying at youth hostels and reaching London perhaps. He could buy all the provisions he wanted for his nuclear shelter, tins of stew and corned beef (not Argentine, of course). He stopped throwing stones at the barrel.

They decided what to do. They would get the barrel to Robert's house, as it was on the road from the village to the beach and slightly nearer than Matthew's. They carried it up to the sea wall, one at each end. It was very heavy, and it was awkward walking sideways on the pebbles. When they reached the top they rested for a while and then started to push it up the road. It was very steep out of the cove and they couldn't let go; they had to keep pushing all the time, bending low. Every now and then they straightened their backs and rested with the barrel held against their legs. It wouldn't roll in a straight line, but wanted to turn to left or right all the time.

It was uphill all the way to Robert's, though it flattened out a bit towards the end. Streaming with sweat and with their backs aching, they manhandled the barrel through the gate and into the front garden. They collapsed on to the grass.

When they had recovered, they asked Mrs James if they could use the phone; Robert was still at school. "Help yourselves," she said. They looked up the local brewers in the directory.

"Who's going to do it?" asked Conan.

"You are," said Matt.

"I'm not doing it."

So Matthew rang the number. "Oh hullo," he said. "I've got an aluminium beer barrel. I wondered if you'd be interested?"

He had to explain that he hadn't bought it, he had in fact — though he hadn't wanted to tell them this — found it in the sea.

He was put through to somebody's secretary and had to repeat the story all over again. Then there was a long wait.

"What's going on?" asked Conan.

"She's gone to ask about it."

Eventually she came back and said they were not interested.

"They don't want to know," said Matthew.

Conan groaned. Their hopes of a small fortune were dashed. After all their hard labour, rolling the barrel uphill for a mile, to be told that it was all for nothing! Then he cheered up a little. "At least, we've still got the beer," he said.

They borrowed some tools from Robert's mum and after a struggle managed to open the keg.

Then they borrowed a tankard. Matthew lifted and poured while Conan held the glass. When it was filled, he held it to the light. It was a good colour.

He took a mouthful. The expression on his face changed and he spat out the drink. He danced about in exaggerated disgust, wiping his lips with his hand.

"What's the matter?" asked Matthew.

"It's bloody sea water," said Conan.

*

HMS *Conqueror* returned from the Falklands. The nuclear-powered submarine sailed into her home port on the Clyde flying the Jolly Roger pirate flag. The officers were on the conning tower and the crew were lined up on the deck below. The flag confirmed for the first time that the submarine had torpedoed the Argentine cruiser *General Belgrano*. Instead of a skull and crossbones, it had a skull and crossed torpedoes, and in a corner of the flag was the symbol of a dagger, showing that it had taken part in a 'cloak-and-dagger' operation, probably the secret landing of a team from the Special Boat Squadron.

Matthew watched the television pictures, and imagined what it would be like, going ashore after dark into enemy territory.

He went to the shoot on Saturday afternoon, for the first time for years. The local gun club owned a stretch of Goosewartha Moors on top of the hill opposite their house and held a clay pigeon shoot there once a month. They had an old GWR van which they used as a clubhouse; inside were the catapults used for launching the 'clay pigeons', which were no more than plastic discs, and a bottled-gas stove on which they brewed tea. In his last year at primary school he used to go to every shoot. He would make himself useful, picking up all the spent cartridges on the ground and recovering any unsmashed discs. The secretary of the club always gave him a pound at the end of the afternoon, but he had never been back since starting at the comprehensive school.

There were several cars parked on the stony ground; it had been levelled by a bulldozer and nothing grew there. About half a dozen men were at a stand, all of them dressed in khaki, green or brown. Matthew did not feel out of place. They all carried guns, most of them broken open, but one man at the stand had his gun to his shoulder.

"Pull," he shouted.

From out of sight the launcher shot two clay pigeons into the air, one hurtling along behind the other on a higher trajectory.

Bang . . . bang, went the gun, as the marksman fired first one barrel and then the other at the flying discs. Each disc seemed to stop short in its flight and explode into fragments, scattering in all directions.

"Good shot," exclaimed a voice.

The secretary recognised Matthew, having seen him around the village in the last five years, even if he hadn't come to the shoot.

"Do you mind if I watch?" Matt asked.

"Of course not," he said.

Matthew felt he was too old now to make himself useful tidying the ground. He stood behind the guns. It was fascinating to see a clay pigeon arrested in its flight and bursting apart, shattering like a star. It was a moment that he could watch again and again.

The men were mostly farmers and businessmen. He listened to them, enjoying their talk of guns and shooting and their banter amongst each other.

"Have you ever handled a gun?" Farmer Trevithick asked him.

"No," said Matthew. He had never had the opportunity, it had never arisen.

"Would you be interested?"

"Yeh," he said.

The farmer explained to him the parts of the gun and

showed him that it wasn't loaded. He warned him never to point it at anyone. Then he handed it to him.

Matthew felt the gun in his grasp, the metal of the double barrel in his left hand, the stock against his side.

"Would you like a go?"

Matt nodded.

They took their turn at the stand and the farmer put a cartridge in each barrel while Matthew held the gun. Then he brought up the barrels until they locked. He raised the gun to his shoulder and looked along the sights. The older man adjusted his position slightly.

"Pull," he shouted.

The clay pigeons flew into the air. Matthew pulled on one trigger and the recoil took him by surprise, the stock of the gun banging back into his right shoulder. The end of the barrel seemed to sweep wildly across the sky, and before he could control it again and squeeze the second trigger both of the plastic discs had fallen unharmed to earth.

He had always secretly thought that clay pigeon shooting must be dead easy. With all that shot spreading over a wide area, he didn't see how anyone could miss. It wasn't like a sharpshooter in a western, who could throw a bottle into the air and shatter it with a single bullet.

"It's the first time," said Farmer Trevithick. "There'd be no skill in it if you could do it straight away." He pushed the gun tighter into Matthew's shoulder and Matthew held it steady where he expected the flight of the discs to pass. He had one cartridge left.

"Pull," shouted the farmer.

Matthew did not try to follow the clay pigeons. He waited until one came into sight and when he thought he was aiming slightly ahead of it, he squeezed the trigger.

It was like a missile hitting a Super-Etendard. The plastic disc suddenly stopped in full flight and, almost in slow motion, almost gracefully, shattered into fragments. The other disc flopped to earth amongst the heather.

"Well done," said Farmer Trevithick. "You'll make a good marksman."

"Thanks," said Matthew, handing back the gun. He held on to the last moment to the feel of the metal of the barrel and the wood of the stock.

"Are you thinking of joining the Army, then?" asked his dad when they were at table, the only time they met as a family.

"I might."

He had not told his parents about going to the Recruiting Office, but he had made no secret of it, leaving the brochures lying around his room, on the desk and bed where they must have seen them. His mother and father looked at each other. He knew they wanted him to stay on at school, to go into the sixth form and then to university. They expected him to follow the path that they had taken, not to leave school at sixteen.

"Why do you want to do that?"

"I dunno."

"You must have a reason."

Matthew squirmed, he did not want to talk about it. "I only enquired," he said. "I thought it might be interesting."

"I wouldn't like you to become a soldier," said his mum, with real distress. "I should be worried about you all the time. You might be killed."

"I might be killed crossing the road."

"I know, I worry about you on your bike."

"If it happens, it happens."

"But there's no need to look for danger." She had stopped eating and stared at him. He dropped his eyes to his plate. "If you had been a soldier you might have been on the *Sir Galahad* when it went up in flames. That was terrible."

In his mind's eye, Matt saw again the television images of the burning ships, the *Sir Galahad* and the *Sir Tristram*, hit by missiles as they waited to land troops at Bluff Cove. He saw the orange flames beneath clouds of billowing black smoke, the helicopters flying in and out of it, using the downdraught of their rotorblades to push inflatable liferafts away from the burning oil on the surface of the water, the burnt and injured men stumbling ashore. It was a risk you had to take.

"Will they take you at sixteen?" asked his dad.

"You can join as a cadet."

"Wouldn't it be better to join later, with a degree? They'll sponsor you through university and you become an officer straight away."

"But I'm not going to get a degree, am I?"

"Why not?"

"Because I'm not even going to get my O levels. I've made a mess of them, haven't I? You've said so yourself."

"We don't know," said his mum. "You might have done quite well."

"I've messed them up, you know I have."

"You could take them again," said his dad. "You're young, you only just got into your age group. With an extra year's experience you'll be all right."

"I don't want to go back to school."

"You can't find a good job at sixteen, you'd be lucky to

find a job at all. If you became a cadet you'd probably stay in the ranks until you'd done your time. And then what future would you have?"

What future does anyone have? thought Matthew.

"If you want a satisfying job that will last a lifetime, you need qualifications. It's true, Matthew."

It was different now, he wanted to say. Nobody could expect a satisfying job that would last a lifetime. Nobody had these vast horizons anymore. But he didn't know how to say it, he didn't know if it was even true.

"You could get them, Matt," his dad was saying. "You're not brilliant —"

Thanks, Dad.

"— but you've got determination, you've always got there in the end. You'll be able to put it right, even if you haven't done very well this time. Don't throw everything away, just because of one setback."

"And we don't even know that it is a setback," said his mum. "We must wait and see."

Wait and see! The holidays were passing and all he did was wait for the examination results. Even the Army wasn't interested in him until he knew his results.

On the television news Matthew listened to Mrs Thatcher's victory speech at Cheltenham. She appealed to the striking train drivers to put their families, their comrades and their country first by continuing to work. She celebrated Britain's victory in the Falklands and linked the achievements of the Task Force with the battle against union militancy at home. Britain, she said, was no longer a nation in retreat. "Yet why does it need a war to bring out our qualities and reassert our pride?" she asked. "Why do we have to be invaded before we throw aside our selfish aims and begin to work together?"

Robert James finished his last exam and they all met on the beach. There were a few more cars in the car park now, and the beach café was open. After a swim, they went for a hot drink. There was a board behind the counter, with all the drinks available and the prices written up in chalk.

"Hot chocolate," read Conan. "We've got to have hot chocolate."

"I can't stand Hot Chocolate," said Matt.

"*It started with a kiss.*"

"Dreadful!"

It was being played almost continuously on Radio One. They started to sing together, "'But then, you were only eight and I had just turned —'". Instead of 'nine', they shouted in chorus "— forty-five!" They laughed so much they had to hold on to each other.

"Do you want hot chocolate or not?" demanded the woman behind the counter, crossly.

"Yes," they said, "we'll have hot chocolate."

And they fell about laughing again. The drink was good, thick and warming after the cold swim.

They went to the farm sale, up the valley from Bluff Cove. It was a warm summer's day (it was mid-winter now in the Falklands, and the expeditionary forces were on their way home). There were cars parked along the side of the road to the village; they glistened in the sun. The first people to arrive had parked in the lane, in the shade of the tall hedges. The farm was halfway down the hill, a slate-roofed, white-walled building with stone barns around it. It lay peacefully in the sunlight. Beyond it a field of dry, brownish grass sloped down to the stream. The other side of the valley was covered with burrows, mine waste where nothing grew.

It was strange to be wandering through the gate into the farmyard. Jimmy Vell had always regarded boys as his natural enemy, and assumed they were up to no good if he saw them on his land. Matt half expected him to come out of one of the barns, waving his stick and roaring at them to clear off. Now it was all laid open and exposed.

The buildings were in a tumbledown condition, with doors falling off their hinges and slates slipping from the roofs. The auctioneers had chalked on the walls of barns: CATTLE ... HAY ... BALES OF STRAW. Inside another barn, where the double doors opened right back, they had set out a table and chairs, facing the yard. There was a tractor and various implements, and piles of tools and equipment laid out in the sun.

The auction had attracted a crowd of people. Some of them were holiday visitors in beach clothes, drawn to the sale out of curiosity. Others were local people who had known Jimmy all their lives. There were women in old-fashioned summer dresses, an old man in a straw hat. Several of the old men looked very small, with shrivelled faces. They wandered around slowly, looking at the heaps of scrap metal, harness, barrels and sacks. A group of women went from barn to barn, shaking their heads. "Oh, the state of the place!" one of them said.

"Enough to keep anyone busy for ten years," said an old man briskly.

There were also several businessmen who stood out from the local people. A few men moved about much more purposefully than the rest, and Matthew recognised the two who had been measuring the field down by the wood at the junction of the two valleys. The older man wore the same brown check suit. He recognised, too, some of the members of the gun club.

The brown-suited man brought Mr Vellanoweth out of the house. The old farmer looked uncomfortably hot, in a heavy pullover and thick trousers tucked into his Wellington boots. He pushed back the cap from his forehead. They were talking very determinedly.

There was a gate out of the yard into the field, and there the boys waited. Conan sat on the top bar, and the other two leaned against it. It was warm in the sun and time seemed to pass slowly. Everything seemed drowsy and timeless. Beyond the gate were the slopes of the valley, the tawny fields, the low trees around the stream further down. Over the top of the hill Matthew could hear the clatter of a mower cutting the hay on the next farm.

The auctioneer stepped into the yard. He took his place behind the table, with Mr Vellanoweth on one side and the solicitor and auctioneer's clerk on the other. He held out his arms like a preacher and invited everyone to come closer. He was a large man in his checked suit, full of bonhomie and confidence. The congregation drew in and Matt, leaning against the gate, wondered which of them would buy the farm. "Jimmy Vell has been a good friend of mine for many years," the auctioneer announced. "It's very sad that the time has come for him to give up farming because of failing health." He changed his tone. "But this is not an occasion for sentiment, ladies and gentlemen. It's a real sale, and I'm sure Jimmy won't mind if I tell you he's put a very realistic reserve on the property."

He introduced the solicitor who would read the Conditions of Sale. The solicitor read a long document in a dry voice. Matthew looked at the two men going about their work. He could not imagine himself doing anything with the same conviction. They seemed to him to be acting. Perhaps that was what happened with all jobs. You pretended to be an auctioneer or a solicitor and eventually you turned into one.

At last the solicitor finished and the auctioneer sprang into action, making the most of the contrast between the dull reading of the legal conditions and the drama of the bidding. With a sense of urgency, he tried to start at fifty thousand pounds. There were no takers.

"Come on now, ladies and gentlemen," he appealed to the audience.

A young man offered thirty-five thousand.

In bids of five thousand pounds, it rose quickly to fifty-five thousand.

There were interruptions from a man the auctioneer addressed as 'Cap'n'. The captain wanted to know who owned the car park. Then he wanted to know whether Gullen Rock was included in the sale and if the owner of the farm was responsible for providing lifeguards.

The auctioneer said it was all specified in the catalogue, and would the 'Cap'n' confine himself to genuine questions. He did not interrupt any more.

The price reached seventy-five thousand pounds. The young man who had been bidding looked despairingly at his wife, and shook his head.

Someone else entered the bidding, and the price rose to a hundred thousand pounds. There was dead silence, and the audience seemed to hold their breath as it went up through the hundred thousands and reached two hundred thousand. It reached two hundred and fifty-five thousand pounds, and there was a pause.

"At two hundred and fifty-five thousand pounds," said the auctioneer. "I offer it once, I offer it twice. . . Gone!" He carried a broken-off cane and brought it down with a great whack across the table.

The crowd seemed to breathe out and relax, and there was a great buzz of conversation. Who had bought the farm? It wasn't the National Trust, they said. Their limit had been a quarter of a million. Who was the new owner? The buyer went forward to sign the contract and all eyes turned towards him. He wasn't a local man, he looked like a holiday visitor. He was very tall and wore a cowboy hat, with a bright floral shirt outside his trousers. His name was passed through the crowd. He was called Weightman, not a local name. The rumour went round that he was Dutch, then that he was American. He was going to turn the farm into riding stables, someone said he was going to use it as a ranch.

"He looks like a bank robber," said Matt.

"He could be," said Robert. "A lot of bank robbers buy property in Cornwall."

"Yeh, a bank robber," said Conan.

A little later they heard one of the women say to the man in the straw hat, "They say he's a bank manager."

Conan nearly fell off the gate, and the other two had to prop him up.

After the sale of the farm, it was the turn of the cattle. While the contract was being signed in the barn, a number of men were pulling gates around the doorway of a cattle shed, to form a pen. A tough, thick-set character in blue shirt and jeans broke open a bale of straw and scattered it on the ground. The auctioneer entered the ring. Jimmy Vell, the new quarter-millionaire, hurried in through the dark doorway with a bowl of corn to feed and settle his animals. "They'll be frightened," he called.

A black and white Hereford cow came out first, pausing suspiciously at the door, surprised by the crowd staring at her. She put down her front legs and pulled her head back. "They're not used to people," shouted Jimmy from inside the shed, pushing the cow from behind. The thick-set man in blue patted her on the rump and kept her moving round and round.

She sold for four hundred and ninety guineas. Next a cow and calf came into the ring, and then the steers. The chickens made one pound and five pence each.

After selling the livestock, the tractor and the farm implements, the auctioneer moved off around the yard, trying to take the crowd with him. But they seemed to lose interest and broke into smaller groups. He beat his cane against a galvanised water tank, producing a hollow, drumming sound. He couldn't get a bid of five pounds for it. "Come on, ladies and gentlemen, I've seen people live in worse."

It went for two pounds. A pile of scrap metal was sold for a pound. A barrel made three pounds, after it had been broken open and found to contain molasses. The gates fetched thirteen pounds each.

He came to a sort of mast, with blocks and tackle and various lengths of rope. It had once been used for building hayricks. "What am I bid for this?" he asked. "Shall we say five pounds?"

Nobody wanted it.

"Three pounds?"

Still no bid.

"One pound then?"

"Fifty pence," shouted Matthew.

"Fifty pence?" repeated the auctioneer. He paused for effect, as though the bid was a joke. A few people laughed. "Sold," he said briskly.

Matthew called out his name, as other buyers had done.

"What did you do that for?" asked Conan, as though Matt had gone off his head.

"I don't know," said Matthew. He had thought that the rope would be useful in the tunnels, but he was as surprised as they were. "It's a bargain."

"We'd better get him away from here," said Robert, "before he buys anything else."

He went to the barn to pay his fifty pence, plus Buyer's Premium and VAT. The people who had been ahead of him in the queue were already loading their purchases. A girl in an Indian cotton dress was throwing scrap metal into a large red caravanette. The farmer who had bought the chickens was carrying them by the legs and putting them into a blue Morris van.

"How are you going to take it away?" asked Robert.

They went across the yard to have a look at the new acquisition. Conan lifted one end of the mast and staggered under its weight, pretending it was much heavier than it was.

"It's all right," said Matthew. "If we take one end each, Robert can carry the ropes."

"Oh, no," said Conan. "I haven't recovered from the barrel yet, my hands have got blisters on them."

"I won't take it home," said Matt. "Just to the adit in the valley."

"That's all," warned Conan.

As they left the farmyard with the huge mast and tackle, they could hear the auctioneer's voice from the front of the house, where he had started to sell the furniture. A cattle lorry backed up to the barn to load the cows.

At first it was not too difficult, through the fields and the lane. It was downhill and the way was straight. They crossed the stream and took the path through the woods where the fox cubs were hidden in the old rabbit burrow. It was about the time of day when the vixens came to visit, but there was no sign of them. They reached the junction with the other valley, and stopped.

To join the footpath through this valley they had to manoeuvre the spar around a right-angled bend. They could not swing it around the corner because of the trees on either side. Matthew held the top of the pole and pushed through the heather and gorse on the hllside until Conan, holding the base, was on the path. Then he swung down through the growth and was carried away by the weight. He crashed through the bracken and fell into the path.

He picked himself up. From here onwards it was all uphill. They struggled up the slope through the fresh green bracken. The mast seemed to get heavier and heavier.

"I've got a splinter," said Conan.

They dropped their load and Robert took the slither of wood out of his finger.

"Come on," said Matthew.

Laboriously they climbed the slope. It was like manoeuvring a field gun into position in the hills west of

Port Stanley before the final assault on the town. At least they weren't under enemy bombardment.

They passed their hide or lookout and the path levelled out along the hillside. When they reached the sycamore tree they eased the spar down through the gorse until it rested in the hollow. They clambered down and used it as a battering ram through the undergrowth to cross the stream and line it up with the entrance to the adit.

Fortunately the tunnel went straight into the hillside and they could take the mast some way inside before the passage curved. They dropped it on the rocky floor and made for the daylight.

"That's it," said Conan, once they were outside. "I'm not doing it again. I'm not going to spend my holiday humping beer barrels and masts around the countryside. It's pointless."

They went into school for a last day. The exams were over for everyone and they had to hand in their books, return the keys of lockers, leave envelopes for their results. It seemed strange being back in school. Matthew felt that he no longer belonged there and yet he didn't belong anywhere else. He only stayed for the morning, riding into the town on his bike at lunchtime, and then home.

That night there was a party to celebrate the end of the exams. It was held at the home of the Williams brothers who lived on a farm a few miles inland. Robert's dad was going to pick them up and take them.

Matthew stood waiting at the back window, watching for a car to pull up at the gate. He had the bottle of wine that he had bought after leaving school inside his zipped-up jacket, a grey blouson. He wore jeans and a tee shirt instead of his khaki.

The car came into view and he rushed for the door, in order not to keep them waiting. "Bye, Mum. Bye, Dad," he shouted. As he crossed the threshold the bottle slipped out of his blouson and smashed on the steps. The glass scattered, the red wine flowed down the drive.

"Oh no," he cried. He could have wept with frustration and annoyance.

His parents came to the door, having heard the crash. "What's happened?" asked his mum, and then she saw the curved pieces of glass and the wine. Robert came up the drive to fetch him.

"Aren't you funny!" said his mum.

It didn't make him feel any better.

"Why did you try to keep it secret? You know we wouldn't mind."

"We'd expect you to take a bottle to a party," said his dad. "It's only normal."

"I wasn't trying to hide it," he said. He hadn't tried to hide it, but he hadn't drawn attention to it either.

"It doesn't matter," said his mum.

He clenched and unclenched his fists. "I'm mad with myself."

"It's not that important."

"It's all right," said Robert. "I've got a bottle of cider, it'll do for both of us."

"I'll give you another bottle," said his dad.

"Shall I clear it up?" he asked.

"No, leave it, I'll see to it," said his mum. She fetched a dustpan, while Matthew and Robert picked up the biggest of the jagged pieces of glass.

His dad came back with a bottle of French wine.

"Don't drop that one."

They went down to the car. He still felt mad with himself, out of all proportion. He wished everyone hadn't been so nice about it. He glanced down at the label on the bottle of claret. It looked much better than the plonk he had bought. It was too good for a school party.

They drove slowly along the unfamiliar and darkening lane, looking for a horse van. It had been parked at the entrance to the farm as a landmark for anyone trying to find the house.

"There it is," said Robert, sitting in the front.

His dad pulled in to the side of the road and they all got out, clutching their bottles. Beyond the horse van was a farmhouse, all the windows ablaze with lights. A boy and a girl were standing outside, but they did not know them. The porch was piled high with sleeping bags, crash helmets and coats. They added their own jackets, and went through the door.

They were in the kitchen, bright with light and noisy with conversation from the crowd of people. They put their drink on a table, with lots of other bottles of cider and wine and cans of beer. A girl from school called Laura picked up Matthew's bottle and looked at it appreciatively. "Look what I brought," she said, pulling a face. "I went to the off-licence and they refused to serve me. I argued with them, said I was over eighteen, and they gave in. It was only when I started drinking that I found out why!" She pointed to a cluster of cans of Barbican alcohol-free beer. "Has anyone got a corkscrew?"

There were several people from school. They all seemed to be asking one another how they got there and how they were getting home.

"I'll just have a look around," said Matthew.

He went through an arch into the main room. It was darker in here and there was music for dancing, though most people were standing around.

He joined a group that he knew; they were talking about school. The fifth formers were asking the sixth formers what it was like in the sixth form, and they were being very responsible about it, as though they had been told to give a good impression of sixth form life.

He reconnoitred the whole of the ground floor. Robert had taken up a position on the stairs, from where he could watch all that was going on. Matthew went back to the kitchen.

He saw Conan's orange hair and pink jumper, through a haze of cigarette smoke. Conan held the bottle of claret and was getting through it rapidly. Laura made him give it to her, and she poured a glass for Matt, before the bottle was empty.

"Where's Debbie?" he asked. She was Laura's friend, they were nearly always together.

"She went to another party," she said. "She hoped Jackson would be there, but he's come to this party. She'll be mad."

He wandered into the main room again. They were talking about exam results. The Government was putting pressure on the examining boards to raise the standards, they said, so that the number going on to further education would be reduced. It was Maggie Thatcher who was behind it. The results this year would be lower by at least a grade.

It was very depressing. He couldn't get away from school and examination results. He sat down on a sofa next to two girls, Rachel from the fifth form and a girl called Caroline who went to an independent school. They compared life at the two establishments: they seemed to be worlds apart.

"What are you going to do?" he asked her.

She wanted to be a doctor. She had it all planned out, she even knew which hospital she wanted to train at. She didn't seem at all worried about her results, unlike everyone else he knew.

The cast of the school play arrived, and the rooms were more crowded than ever. After the production they had been to a teacher's house and then come on to the party. The teacher with them went around saying to everyone, "What are *you* doing here?" as though she was surprised to see them.

It was a good question. He wondered what he *was* doing there. It didn't seem much of a celebration to talk about results and what they were going to do in the future.

The music was turned up loud and it became impossible to talk. More people began to dance. There was an alarm when someone started the horse van and tried to drive it away. Matthew followed several others outside. Trevor Williams pulled the driver out of the cab and placed him on the verge. In the road a girl was hitting a boy. "Go on, hit me back!" she screamed. "I can't reach your back," he shouted.

The air was fresh after the crowded rooms. Matt found he was standing next to Conan. He was talking to him when suddenly Conan stopped answering, in mid-sentence. He turned around and Conan had vanished. He felt puzzled by his disappearance and then in the darkness heard groans. He looked down and

Conan was lying on the ground.

He sat him up and pushed his head between his knees. When Conan had recovered, he left him sitting on the grass bank next to the boy who had tried to drive the van away. He went across the road and climbed a gate into a field, to have a pee. He was startled when a boy and a girl jumped up out of the long grass.

The lights blazed from the house and the music blared. The Williams brothers threw out Jackson, who staggered down the road. Matthew helped Conan back inside. In all the commotion and noise, the dancing and drink, the exams were forgotten.

They met on the beach next day at the usual spot, high up on the rocks at one side. It was where the boys from the village had always gathered. The cliff behind them was covered with initials and dates carved into the stone. The earliest dated from the beginning of the century and there were others from every decade since. Robert could point out several of his relatives. There was an A.J. 07 who was his great-uncle. He had carved his initials in the same year that he had swum to Gull Island. The family had a photograph of him taken after he came out of the water, a wiry little man in a bathing costume of horizontal stripes that covered him from his shoulders to his knees. He had been killed in France during the First World War.

At one time all the local boys used to swim around the island. It was something you were more or less expected to do, once in your lifetime. Nobody did it any more since the council had provided the lifeguard service.

After the party, they felt too lazy to swim. They had each selected a space on the wall of rock that rose from their ledge to the cliff top, and were adding their own initials to the collection. All the best places had already been taken. Robert was standing, Matthew kneeling, Conan sitting cross-legged nearby.

It would take the whole summer, perhaps several seasons, to carve as deep as the old ones. Some from the fifties and sixties were already wearing away and were too faint to be legible.

As he worked, Matt thought of the girl at the party, how she seemed to know just what her future would be. It had impressed him a lot. "What are you going to do?" he asked Conan.

"I'll finish this T."

"I don't mean now, stupid. I mean . . . in life!"

"Life," echoed Conan vaguely, as though he didn't know what it was.

"It's what happens after O levels," said Robert.

"You mean there's something more?" He refused to take it seriously.

Robert wanted to study Biology at A level, but he did not have much idea after that. When Matthew pressed him, he said he would like to work his way around the world. Conan thought the Merchant Navy would be all right, but then he changed his mind.

"Matt's going to join the Army," he said. "I saw him coming out of the Recruiting Office. He's had an interview."

"Have you?" asked Robert. "What did they want to know?"

"They asked him which corps he wanted to join," said Conan. "And he said 'Um, er . . . the apple core'."

Both boys laughed.

"They thought 'We've got a smart lad here'."

"Officer material, obviously."

"Aw, shut up," said Matthew. "It wasn't an interview. I just picked up some leaflets, I haven't applied yet."

"Are you going to?"

"I might."

With his red-handled Swiss army knife, he scraped away at the final downstroke of the M. He wanted his initials to be as deep and as bold as Arthur James's, he wanted them to last as long. He realised what time and effort Robert's great-uncle must have put into making his mark. It was easy to scratch your initials and date on the rock; what took time was making an incision a quarter of an inch deep.

It was a pity it was the summer of '82, he thought. The date was hard to carve with all its curves. The last easy year was '77, there wouldn't be another easy one until '11. Twenty thousand and eleven! He'd be forty-five years old then, like the man in their song.

He couldn't imagine himself at forty-five, what he'd be like or what he'd be doing. He didn't really believe it would ever happen.

At the weekend he watched, on television, the return of the *Canberra* from the Falklands. The huge white P&O liner was stained with rust after her journey to the South Atlantic. As she came up the Solent, she was surrounded by a swarm of small boats sounding fog-horns and sirens. Helicopters roared overhead. The men on board, the Third Commando Brigade of the Royal Marines, shouted and sang. A girl in a speedboat took off the top of her bikini and waved it at the troops.

The quayside was crowded with people, swarming

over the cranes and the roofs of warehouses. They waved
flags and cheered, and held up posters saying WEL-
COME HOME, FRED ... WELCOME HOME,
SPUD. The marines unfurled banners from the side of the
boat: RULE BRITANNIA ... WE WENT, WE
FOUGHT, WE CONQUERED ... LOCK UP YOUR
DAUGHTERS, THE BOOTNECKS ARE BACK!
They craned over the side of the ship to try and recognise
wives and relatives in the thousands of up-turned faces,
and they waved and shouted when they saw someone
they knew. The Prince of Wales arrived by helicopter.

"What about the ones who aren't coming back?"
asked his mum. "How do their wives and mothers feel?"

But she could not spoil it for Matthew. The scenes on
television, live at first and then repeated in every news
programme, revived all his excitement. For the next few
days he pored over all the newspaper photographs of the
marines' triumphant return from war. In his bedroom he
studied again the leaflets that he had collected from the
Army Recruiting Office, with their pictures of soldiers
building bridges, firing guns and driving tanks.

Conan came running out of the sea, fluffing up his hair.
"Is it all right?" he asked. "Is it in spikes?"

"It's great."

He ran on to the bar and wrote VERUCCAS in the
sand, the six foot high letters facing up the beach towards
anyone arriving on the sea wall. He had given up writing
BAD BRAINS since he had bought their record and
found that half of it was reggae. They dried themselves on
the rocks and lay on their towels in the sun.

Conan wanted to start a group. He and Robert could

strum on the guitar a bit. They thought Matthew could play the drums, anyone could do it. Matt said he'd have a go if they provided the instruments.

"What are we going to call ourselves?"

Conan ran through the names of a few groups: Sexgang Children; Blitz; Even Worse; Christians In Search Of Filth; Meat Puppets.

"All of them wonderful, to coin a John Peel word," said Robert.

They thought of a few, but none of them had the authentic ring.

"What about The Bootnecks?" asked Matthew.

"That's brilliant," said Robert. "I like the pun."

"What pun?" asked Conan.

"The beatniks of the fifties."

Matt hadn't realised the play on words either, but he was pleased to take credit for it.

"How did you think of it?" asked Robert.

"It just came to me," he said modestly.

So the group was to be called The Bootnecks. They lay in the sun, talking about their plans and the music they'd heard on the radio last night. They all listened to John Peel's choice of records each evening from ten to midnight. They talked more about the things he said, like having his photo taken for the Radio One calendar, than about the music. He chose some very obscure records, but they preferred these to the ones in the charts, like Hot Chocolate and Dexy's Midnight Runners, which was Number One all summer.

"We'll write our own songs," said Conan.

"What about?"

It wasn't easy. They made up some lyrics about waiting for examination results, hanging around just filling in the time, expecting the worst. Conan thought it was too ordinary, but he didn't come up with anything better.

From time to time the clouds obscured the sun. They would feel cold and sit up, and think of getting dressed. Then the sun would shine again and they would immediately feel warm. It was a bright, windy summer.

"Hey, look at this!" shouted Robert.

He was standing on the seaward side of the bar, at his feet a heap of what looked like rubbish. Matthew splashed over to him.

"What is it?" he asked. "More plastic?" The pile was made up of colourless discs.

"No, they're alive," said Robert. "They're By-the-Wind Sailors, they're a sort of jellyfish. The wind fills these sails and blows them along. They've drifted all the way from the South Atlantic."

Matthew's interest was caught by the mention of the South Atlantic. They had made the same journey as the ships of the Task Force returning from the Falklands. There ought to have been crowds lining the beach, cheering and waving flags. There ought to have been bands playing *Rule Britannia*, and topless girls waving their bras.

"Their proper name is *velella velella*," said Robert, rather apologetically.

A wave fringed with white foam surged up the slope of the bar and swept them along sideways, spreading them out in a glistening line and returning some to the sea.

They spent the afternoon in Robert's bedroom, trying to

create their own sound. Conan and Robert struck chords on their guitars, shouting any of the lines that they could remember from the beach or making up fresh ones as they came into their heads. Matthew banged the Irish Breweries beer barrel until they could find him a proper set of drums. He beat out any sort of rhythm, just letting himself go and behaving like a drummer on a video. Perhaps if he pretended to be a drummer he would become one.

It was their own sound all right, nobody else could have made anything like it. It was dreadful, but they laughed a lot. And towards the end of the session there were a few minutes when it seemed to lift off, and they forgot that they were just playing around. Then the door opened and Mrs James looked in. The sounds tailed away.

"What a noise!" she exclaimed good-humouredly. "You'll make yourselves deaf."

"Wait till we get the electrics," said Robert. They all laughed in embarrassment.

"Why don't you take over the shed?" she suggested. "You could make as much noise as you want there."

They thought of improvements to their song, to make it more pointed. It wouldn't be just about waiting, it would be about how the Government was going to doctor the results, how there would be more young people unemployed. But once Robert's mum had interrupted, they could not believe in it in the way they had before. Somehow she had broken the spell.

Robert's dad had once had a market garden and there was an old packing shed he no longer used. They took it over for rehearsals. They wanted to get some tee shirts with the name of the group, so that they could all wear the same. It was too expensive to get them printed, but they could buy some plain ones quite cheaply and print them themselves.

"The Art department has got some special paint," said Matt.

They were reluctant to go into school again.

"I don't mind going," said Matthew. "I don't mind asking."

He collected a couple of pounds from each of them and next morning he rode into school, where the term had still not finished. He thought of his disastrous exam painting of South Georgia as he walked down the corridor into the Art block.

The teacher said he had no suitable paint, so he rode into town and bought three plain tee shirts reduced to a pound each because they were seconds, and a pot of the special cloth paint. They spent several mornings making various designs, then cutting stencils out of cardboard and applying the paint. They ironed them to make them permanent, according to the instructions, and washed and dried them.

It was a great moment when they all put them on, with a lot of laughing and joking. They had become very involved in the production of The Bootnecks tee shirts. They hadn't spent much time practising the song.

In the afternoons, they were mostly on the beach. The bar, that summer, built up higher than it had ever been before, a bank of sand across the mouth of the cove. It created a shallow lagoon at the top of the beach, beneath the sea wall and the pebbles. The stream from the valley flowed over rocks and stones into the far side of the lagoon, and escaped to the sea through a gap in the sandbank immediately below their vantage point. The water continually ate away at the sand until the edges collapsed and were washed out to sea. The next high tide brought the sand back to rebuild the bank, the salt water swirled into the pool. The boys spent a lot of time watching this process of destruction and renewal, waiting for a miniature cliff of wet sand to split and fall. They would decide which would be the next piece to slip, and cheer as it flopped into the current.

The sand on the seaward side of the bar, on which the Atlantic rollers spent their force, was also higher than usual, burying the rocks and changing the contours of the beach. To Matthew the cliffs seemed less high than other years, their vantage point closer to the shore.

"It must be six metres deep in places," said Robert. "It must be smothering all the limpets on the rocks. It's more of a disaster than a major oil spillage, and yet nobody notices because it's sand instead of oil."

"There's nothing you can do about it," said Conan.

It made no difference to the surfers. They were now on the beach in force, riding the waves or lying around on the sea wall outside the lifeguard's hut. Matthew talked to them, the ones he knew like Mark Clark. Mark had a Hawaiian wetsuit with a pattern of palm trees, and wore surfbeads made of clay. He was said to wash his hair in washing powder to give it a sun-bleached look. He was always boasting about what he had done. The surfers never talked about anything but surfing, about wetsuits and surfboards and waves. Conan sometimes did an imitation of a beachbum. "Hey, that's a good tube, man!" he would say. "Hey, goofy foot, I like your baggies, I like your splats." They had their own language, they lived in a world of their own.

Print-out was one of the hangers-on. As Matthew came over the sea wall after his swim, he came zooming down the road into the car park on his skateboard. He turned and stopped, abruptly and expertly, alongside him. "Hi," he said.

Matt knew him slightly from school, where he was in the same year, although he did not know his proper name. They had given him his nickname because of his clothes. There was a firm called Print-out Promotions which advertised in the *New Music Express*, and he must have ordered his whole outfit from them, the rising-sun tee shirt and the bondage trousers with zips and straps.

They exchanged a few remarks about the condition of the waves, the waiting for results.

"What are you going to do?" asked Matthew.

"I'm going on the dole," said Print-out. He did not mind what his results were, he wanted to go on the dole and buy a secondhand surfboard and spend all his time surfing. "What about you?"

"I don't know," said Matt. "I'll just wait and see."

Print-out started to move, gliding easily down the rest of the slope and turning with a flourish before the stream.

Matthew crossed the stepping-stones and made his way up the valley. The hillsides were turning purple with heather. He passed the wood and started up the slope. He walked with his head down, thinking.

The beachbums knew what they wanted, he thought. There was something to be said for just giving up and enjoying yourself. But he did not know that he could do it, anymore than he believed he could become an auctioneer or a solicitor or a bank manager.

Suddenly he was aware of an obstruction on the path ahead of him. He stopped and looked up. A few metres away an animal coming down the path had stopped and was staring at him. It was one of the fox cubs, its fur red, its ears pricked up. It looked at him curiously with bright blue eyes. It showed no fear, only interest.

For about a minute they watched each other. For Matthew there was a sense of encounter, a feeling of amazement that this creature of the wild shared the same world and survived in it. Then the cub turned and walked back up the path a few paces, revealing its thin body and long bushy tail, before turning into the bracken and slipping away between the tall stalks. It followed a rabbit trail down towards the stream.

As soon as he got home, Matthew phoned Robert to tell him about the cub. Robert had continued to watch them most evenings, and said that the vixens were still visiting the den in the wood. He said that when they came out into the field, two of the cubs never went far from their mother but one was much more adventurous, roaming away to forage for its own food. This was most likely the one that Matthew had seen.

"Is it a male?" asked Matt.

"Probably," said Robert. He could not be quite sure, but the male was usually more adventurous.

"What will they do?" asked Matthew. "I mean, what will happen to them?"

"The females stay in the area where they were born," said Robert. "The males usually move away."

They started going in the autumn and travelled long distances, sometimes as much as a hundred miles, to find new territory.

*

HMS *Hermes*, the flagship of the Falklands Task Force, steamed up the Solent past huge crowds on Portsmouth Hard. They waved their flags, and girls on yachts and motor launches waved the tops of their bikinis. Balloons floated in the air and a Fairey Swordfish flew past, followed by a Victor bomber trailing its refuelling nozzle in front of an arrowhead of three Harrier jet fighters. Relatives on the quayside cheered wildly as the men came down the gangplank, to embrace their wives and to see babies they had never perhaps seen before.

The schools were on holiday, and suddenly the special, privileged part of his summer was over, the part where everyone else was still at school and only he and his class were free to do as they liked. Where had it gone? It had been going to last an immense length of time. He had intended doing all the things he had sacrificed for the exams. He had been going to get into training again for cycle racing. He had been going to tour on his bicycle, wandering from place to place while the countryside was still fairly quiet and the roads free of holiday traffic. He had been going to explore the mine system in the hillsides of the valley and build himself a hideaway deep underground. He had been going to make himself as fit as a commando.

He had done none of it. He had got up late every day and lazed around the beach. He had simply waited for time to pass until the results were out, when he knew already what they would be. He had spent a lot of time printing tee shirts and banging a drum for The Bootnecks, but what they achieved was laughable. They would never succeed as a group, they didn't even have the same taste in music. He was forced to revise his theory, that if you pretend something long enough you will eventually become it. However long they pretended to be a group, they'd never be the real thing. Whatever they did, they were just a bunch of kids messing about.

And now half of his precious time had gone and he was just on holiday like anyone else. He had to do *something*, he kept telling himself. He thought of the men on the *Hermes*, the crowds who welcomed them. He felt restless, frustrated. He wanted action.

He got up earlier the next morning, even before his parents were awake. He put his beach things in the haversack, with his trainers and a torch, the sort with a dome on top that could rest on the floor. He fetched a walking stick from the hallstand and a pickaxe and a shovel from one of the outbuildings, and set off down the valley in sweater, camis and Wellington boots.

It seemed quite different at this time of day. The light had a clear, early-morning quality. Everything was very still and quiet. He felt that he was the only person around.

He let the tools slide down the bank and lowered himself after them, breaking the spiders' threads that stretched between the gorse bushes. The chill of the air inside the adit caught his breath. The noise of stones displaced by his feet echoed in the confined space. He could hear the drip of water.

He shone his torch along the length of the spar, its varnished surface glistening with moisture. The lengths of rope had been dusty when they left the farmyard, but they were now wet to touch, staining his hand with red mud.

He swept the beam around the walls and roof. The tunnel was cut roughly out of the rock. It was not quite vertical, but sloped to one side; he could just stand upright if he kept close to the left-hand wall. Both walls were jagged, with ledges and crevices down which the water dropped, staining the rock with greens and browns.

He moved further into the tunnel, shining the light on the ground and prodding it with his stick to make sure that it was solid. There could be a shaft. If it was flooded and covered with floating débris it would look like a continuation of the floor. The greatest danger would be if it was at an angle, because anyone falling in would tumble down the slope and then rise vertically, trapped underwater beneath the overhanging rock.

The floor of the passage was uneven. It seemed to go horizontally into the hillside, but it probably sloped upwards a little, to allow the water to drain. He tapped his way forward, swinging his light from side to side.

At this distance from the entrance there were no ferns growing in the cracks. The walls of the tunnel were black and running wet. It smelt musty, pungent as vinegar. Suddenly the roof opened up above him into a dark empty space whose limits were out of sight. He checked the floor carefully, to see whether the opening continued below, but it seemed quite safe. He stepped beneath the hole and shone his torch up into a great church-like cavern. There were steps and ledges, pulpits of rock; a few iron bars were driven into the sides. He couldn't see how far it stretched, for the beam of his torch failed to reach the end. He moved it around the sides, to get the enormous scale of the place. He thought of the miners swarming up the bars and over the ledges, hammering the drills into the rock, the ore crashing into the level.

He went on further. He saw two round holes drilled into the wall and felt inside, to see if there were any traces of explosive. He sniffed his fingers; they smelt mouldy and damp, just like everywhere else.

The character of the rock changed. It seemed greyer and more crumbly. There was a pit prop lying on the floor. He stepped on it and the heel of his boot squelched right through the rotten wood. There were a few props in position, though they must have been as soft as the one that had fallen.

Then he came to a roof-fall. A heap of earth and rubble blocked the way, though there was a gap above it through which he might have just been able to crawl. He shone the torch into it, and saw that it stretched some distance. He would try it one day, but not on his own.

He went back to his tools and ropes near the entrance. He began by levelling the floor of the tunnel, clearing any loose stones and putting them into a pile. He would need to make a wall across the front, thick enough to withstand the blast that follows an explosion and to keep out radiation. The best place for the refuge would be in the cavern. He tried to improve the steps up into it, attacking the rock with a pickaxe. It made very little impression. He thought of how long it took to carve his initials in stone. At that rate it would take ages to improve the access to the shelter, to shape sleeping platforms and living spaces.

He looked at his water-resistant watch with the blue, revolving rim: it was nearly eleven o'clock. Conan and Robert would be arriving on the beach. They would probably be having a drink at the café. He could do with a hot chocolate.

Before he left, he had an idea. He changed into his trainers for the beach, and carried his Wellington boots back along the tunnel to the rock-fall. With the shovel he dug out some of the rûbble and placed the two boots sticking out at the bottom of the pile, the toes turned upwards and facing slightly out. He threw the rubble he had removed over them and as a final touch left the walking stick lying casually by the side.

Outside again, he found that he was shivering after three hours underground, despite his sweater. He stood in the patchy sunlight near the stream and took several deep breaths, replacing the damp air in his lungs with the fresh breeze off the sea.

They were carving their names deeper in the rock. "Where have you been?" asked Robert.

"I made a start on the shelter," said Matt.

They were not impressed.

A storm cloud was approaching over the sea. It came in like an invading force of helicopters. It passed the island and came straight for the shore.

Now that the school holidays had begun, there were more people on the beach. None of them seemed to be aware of impending disaster. They were sheltering behind their windbreaks, lying in the sun or brewing tea on camping stoves. Suddenly the attack came, and raindrops spattered like machine-gun bullets on to the sand.

From the side of the cliffs the boys watched as the people reacted. They all started, and looked up. They hurriedly began gathering their things together. For a moment there was panic as the rain increased and the storm lashed the beach. They ran for shelter, to the caves or to their cars. A few wrapped themselves in plastic and dug themselves in. Within minutes the beach was cleared.

The boys enjoyed the spectacle, and then realised that they were getting wet themselves.

"Come up to the adit," Matthew suggested.

"We'd be soaked before we got there," said Conan.

They sheltered in the cave. The storm cloud passed and people gradually returned to the beach. Life carried on as normal.

"Come on," said Matthew. "Come and see the adit."

"I'm not doing any work," warned Conan.

"No," Matt promised.

The rocks were wet and uncomfortable, and there was nothing better to do. They walked up the valley and down the slope to the entrance.

"It's a solid floor," said Matthew. Conan took the torch and led the way.

They passed the hollowed-out cavern and came to where the rock changed. Matthew kept behind.

Suddenly Conan stopped. "Oh my God!" he exclaimed. The other two pressed forward, and in the light of the torch saw where the roof had caved in, burying the figure of a man. Only his boots showed beneath the rubble.

"Oh no!" breathed Robert.

It looked terribly convincing. Even Matthew felt alarmed for a moment.

"Dad," he said reproachfully. "I told you not to come down here on your own."

"Get him out!" shouted Robert. The beam of light flashed across the walls and roof as Conan rushed forward. For a second everything went black as he put the torch on the ground and switched from the beam to the dome. Then the light diffused upwards, casting grotesque shadows on the walls.

Robert was tearing with his hands at the heap of rubble. Conan joined him, lifting stones away from the area just above the boots. One boot came free, then the other. Both were empty.

They turned and saw Matthew grinning at them.

"What's going on?" asked Conan.

"You idiot," said Robert. "You stupid idiot."

"Did *you* do it?" asked Conan.

Matthew nodded.

"You bloody fool." Conan threw the boot he was holding straight at him, catching him in the chest. He doubled over. Robert hurled the other boot.

"It was only a joke," cried Matthew.

They came for him. He turned and ran into the darkness, feeling for the walls. They followed, the light swinging in Conan's hand and their shadows filling the tunnel. They picked up the boots and threw them again, hitting Matthew in the back. He stumbled on the uneven floor.

He saw daylight ahead. He passed the mast, rope and tools, and burst out into the fresh air. "Leave off," he called to the others, as they came menacingly towards him.

They lowered the Wellington boots, and began to laugh. "I really thought it was your dad," said Conan.

"I didn't think you'd be taken in."

"It could have given us a heart attack."

"I thought it was obvious, with the toes turned upwards. Nobody would fall on their back." It had looked like a caricature, a sort of Charlie Chaplin figure.

"We could try and catch someone else," said Conan. "We could get Print-out."

"No," said Matthew. He had lost interest in it now. And anyway, he had had another idea, that had come to him that morning between leaving the adit and going down to the beach. He knew how he would use the mast that he had bought at the sale. He felt that he had really known from the moment of his bid, but it was only now that he had put it into words. It was still vague, it would take the rest of the summer to plan it properly and put it into execution. But at the moment it seemed a brilliant idea.

Suddenly Conan threw the boot at him again. Matthew caught it and passed it to Robert. They threw it to and fro until it fell into the bottom of the depression. As it was Matthew's boot, he had to fetch it himself. He stepped gingerly down into the bowl beneath the sycamore, thinking of the fragile plug of earth and roots that separated him from a fall of a hundred fathoms.

It was now the height of the season and the beach was crowded with holidaymakers. The bar was covered with windbreaks, smothered beneath canvas in red, yellow and orange stripes. The lagoon was filled with rubber dinghies. Normally the lifeguards would not allow any dinghies in the sea, because of the danger of being swept away by the wind and the current. The sheltered water of the pool was ideal for them and the numbers increased daily. The boys counted a dozen, then seventeen, then twenty-three. "It'll be packed solid," they said. "You won't see any water, you'll be able to walk all the way across."

They resented the summer visitors. Earlier in the season they had had the beach to themselves. They had thought of it as theirs, and now it had been invaded by hundreds of foreigners. They retreated to their ledge on the side of the cliff and watched the invaders, passing comments on their looks and behaviour.

They amused themselves by giving names to them. Anyone in the latest fashion — that summer it was pleats and tiered skirts — was a 'plastic'. Anyone who looked boring was an 'anorak'. They divided the beach into degrees, and directed each other's attention to anything of interest. "At eighty degrees near the blue windbreak, someone's just dropped an ice cream into the sand, ha ha!" "At ten degrees coming over the seawall, a girl in a striped tee shirt." "I've got a name for her," said Conan. "What is it?" "It's 'redwhiteredwhiteredwhiteblue'." It was the best invention of the day.

"Here comes the bomb disposal squad," said Matthew, as the stout man with earphones and metal detector searched the beach for lost coins.

They watched the families on holiday. They all seemed to mark out their own little territory on the beach and everyone kept to the rules, not intruding into anyone else's space. In its own space, each family ignored everyone else as though they were the only ones on the beach, carrying on with their business of changing clothes beneath huge towels and eating and drinking. Some families came with four windbreaks which they staked into the sand in a square, and then added a canopy over the top, sitting on the beach in the middle of a pile of canvas. The boys were delighted whenever they discovered one of these.

Robert had a theory that if there was a teenage girl in a

family, she would eventually go off and sit on her own. It would almost certainly be close to the water.

"Go on, now's your chance," he said, as a girl in a ra-ra skirt went and sat on a rock with her feet splashing in the pool. "Go and talk to her."

"No," said Conan. He claimed that only one per cent of girls were good-looking and none of them lived in Cornwall. The only good-looking girls would be amongst the holiday visitors. He went to the beach to find the one per cent, but they were never there. "I wonder if we ought to go to Stennack Cove," he would say. "I wonder what's going on at Stennack."

It became a sort of catchphrase of the summer, that he repeated several times every day. But they never went to the other beach, on the sheltered side of the headland, close to the village.

"There's a one per cent," said Matt.

"Where? Where?" cried Conan.

"Down on the sand, at thirty degrees, near the yellow and orange umbrella."

A young man came over the pebbles and joined the girl.

"Oh no," groaned Conan. "She's got a gorilla in tow."

"At a hundred and ten degrees, almost hidden by the red windbreak," said Robert. "Two girls have come out into the open."

"I can't see them," said Conan.

"There." Robert pointed with his arm.

The girls waved back.

All three boys waved wildly. They kept watching the girls across the crowded, multicoloured beach. The breeze blew in from the sea, high clouds passed overhead. The girls stared back.

After a while the girls got up from the family enclosure

and sauntered across the beach. They went down to the sea's edge and paddled in the shallow water, running back from the waves. They did not look at the boys again. They sat on a rock, their backs towards them.

"They're waiting for you to join them," said Robert.

"Are you coming, Matt?" asked Conan.

"If you want."

Matthew and Conan stood up, casually, as though they were stretching their legs, then climbed down over the rocks. The girls knew they were approaching.

Matt stood in front of them, to one side, while Conan hung back.

"Are you on holiday?" he asked. "Are you at school? Are you doing CSE or O level? Are you waiting for your results?" It always came back to that, whatever he wanted to talk about. They talked about school and exams, and what they were going to do. Conan didn't say a word.

Eventually the boys went down to the sea and kicked water at each other. When they were both soaking wet, they went back to their place on the rocks by a circuitous route.

"You weren't much use," complained Matt, when they were with Robert again. "Why didn't you speak to them?"

"They weren't one per cent," said Conan.

The Bootnecks gave up rehearsing and spent nearly all of their time on the beach. Matthew, too, had abandoned his plan to make the cavern habitable. It was too gloomy working there alone and progress was too slow; he admired all the more the old miners who had cut through the stone with just hammer and drill and their own strength. The cavern would still be there if it were ever needed, and at the moment the beach was more attractive.

But he had not abandoned his other plan, though he had not yet worked it out in detail. Whatever he did, he would need the help of the others, and he was more cautious now about asking them. He waited for the right opportunity.

They were lying on the rocks in the warm sun, looking across at the opposite hillside, covered with heather and grass. Each day riders from the stables trekked along the ridge; the figures looked tiny in the vast landscape. They watched out for them and gave them names, the Troublesome Three, the Famous Five, the Magnificent Seven. A single horse and rider appeared on the horizon, silhouetted against the sky. They looked at each other. "The Lone Ranger," they all said together.

One by one they set about deepening their initials. None of them yet showed up as strongly as A.J. 07.

"Do you realise something?" asked Matt, scraping away at the curves of the date.

"What?"

"It's seventy-five years since A.J. swam to Penguin Island."

"Penguin?" repeated Robert scornfully. "There are no penguins in Cornwall."

"Gull Island, then. Don't you think we ought to mark the anniversary in some way?"

"How?"

"We could swim there ourselves."

The lifeguards would never allow it. They would have to go in the evening. It would be dark before they returned. It would be too dangerous, on their own in the night. They would have to have a support vessel, and then it would become public. The surf life-saving club would take it over. If they did the swim, they wanted to keep it to themselves.

They liked the idea. Robert was interested in celebrating his great-uncle's achievement by repeating it three-quarters of a century later. They were all good swimmers, and were sure that they could cover the distance.

As they climbed over the pebbles to leave the beach, a girl came on to the sea wall. For a moment she and Conan stood face to face, neither able to proceed unless one of them stood aside. She wore a red and white striped skirt tied at the waist with a red cord, and a red tee shirt with the words *I've made up my mind* across it in fairground-style lettering.

"What about?" asked Conan, before he could stop to think.

"Jesus," she said.

"Christ!" said Conan.

"That's right," said the girl.

Matthew and Robert rolled about with laughter. "You've done it, Conan," they said, on their way to the beach café. "You've spoken to a girl at last."

The breeze was filled with the smell of suntan lotion, stronger even than the salt of the sea. They breathed it in as they came over the sea wall, and saw that the tide was in. The holidaymakers were crammed into the space beneath the wall and on the rocky sides of the beach. Their ledges with the initials were occupied by several families.

They climbed the hillside and looked down into the cove. From above, the cars packed tight in the small car park looked like toys, the sun reflecting from the many-coloured roofs. The grey pebbles had disappeared beneath a mass of reds, yellows and blues: it looked as though the confetti colours had been deposited there by the sea and splashed on the sides of the cliffs. All these bright colours were confined within the bottom of the valley, and the hills around were khaki, touched with purple, green and fawn. The sea was a clear blue, edged with the white of the waves; from this distance, they broke silently.

They sat just beneath an outcrop of rock, sheltered from the gusty wind, and made up fantasies. They put piranha fish into the pool, amongst all the dinghies and paddlers. They strafed the beach with rocket-fire, and then attacked it with assault ships and marines.

They cleared it of all the holidaymakers.

It was just as frustrating in the sea. They swam as much as they could, whenever the red flag was not flying, to get into training for the swim to the island. But the lifeguards herded the swimmers into such a small area that they could only thresh around like fish in a net. As soon as they strayed out towards the open water, the guard blew his whistle and called them back. It made the empty spaces of the ocean seem all the more inviting, calling them to strike out towards the island on the horizon.

They climbed back to their rock, clear now of

intruders, and lay in the sun to dry.

"Did you hear John Peel last night?"

"Yeh."

"He had his bike stolen."

"He's got a new one now."

"It's a Holdsworth!"

There was nothing in the news these days. There had been nothing about the Falklands since the return of the Fleet and the service of thanksgiving in Westminster Abbey.

"I'm going to ride more," said Matthew. "It's a good way of training, it uses the same muscles as swimming."

"What I don't understand," said Conan, "is how anyone will know we've done it."

When Arthur James swam around Gullen, it was a Sunday and there were crowds lining the cliffs. They all came down to the cove to watch him come ashore.

"They'll never believe us," said Robert. "They'll think we made it up."

"We've got to leave proof," said Matthew. "We've got to take the mast and set it up at the top of the island and fly a flag from it. Then everyone next morning will see it."

"How do we get it there?" asked Conan, remembering its weight when they carried it up the valley.

"It'll float in the water," said Matthew. "We can tow it. Once we get it down to the beach it'll be easy."

They pictured the island with the tall mast at the top and a flag flying stiffly in the breeze.

"It would be a good joke," said Matthew.

There was an image from the Falklands War that impressed Matthew deeply. It was a photograph of paratroopers, heavily laden and carrying guns at the ready, yomping in single file across a desolate moorland. The man at the rear, nearest to the camera, had a radio aerial sticking up from his pack, and flying from the aerial, standing out straight in the wind, was a Union Jack.

"Where can we get a flag from?" he asked. There ought to have been plenty around from the victory celebrations, but he did not know anyone who had one. It needed to be very large.

"Which flag?" asked Robert.

"The Union Jack, of course." He had never considered anything else.

"Why not the Cornish flag?"

Matthew tried to picture it, but it seemed wrong. He could only see a Union Jack flying from the masthead when they captured the island.

"It belongs to England anyway," said Robert. "There'd be more point flying the Cornish flag and claiming it for Cornwall, especially now it's been sold."

"Why not a skull and crossbones?" said Conan. "Why not our own flag, with *The Bootnecks* on it?"

"It wouldn't show up."

"The Cornish flag would show up best of all."

Matthew felt unhappy. It was beginning to be like the group all over again, everyone with different ideas and their enthusiasm fading away after the first interest. "We're going to do this," he said. It wasn't like talking about putting piranhas in the swimming pool, this was real.

He came back from a long training ride. He was forcing his bike up the steep drive to the back of the house, standing on the pedals and putting all his weight first on one side and then on the other, when the door opened and his mother called. "Matthew, there's a phone call for you."

He extricated his feet from the toe-straps, which was not easy on the slope, put his bicycle on to the ground and ran on tiptoe — because of his cycling shoes — towards the door. "Who is it?" he asked.

"It's Robert," his mum said. "It's lucky I caught you, I was just going to put the phone down."

It was dark inside the house after the brightness outside, and he stumbled into the chairs and table before reaching the phone. "Robert?" he asked.

"Have you seen down the valley?" His voice was urgent.

"No, I've been riding."

"There's a bulldozer, it's knocking down the wood."

"Why?" asked Matthew. He could not understand. The wood had always been there. Why would anyone want to clear it?

"It's the new owner."

"But it's mad."

"I know."

"What can you do about it?"

"Tell everyone you know," said Robert. "Get them to go down there."

They arranged to meet at the junction of the two valleys as soon as possible. He told his mother what was happening and changed out of his cycling gear. Within a few minutes he was running along the footpath and through the tunnel between the hawthorns. He came out on to the hillside and reached the top of the slope down to the wood. In the field below was a yellow bulldozer, its scoop raised in the air like open jaws. The ground had been churned to mud in which its tracks were imprinted, criss-crossing to and fro. The bushes and scrub at the side of the stream had been pushed into a heap, but most of the wood was still intact.

Matthew ran down the path and met Robert coming through the other valley. "I was in the hide waiting for the cubs to come out," he said. "A dumper truck came down from the farm, followed by the bulldozer. It started on the top end of the wood, and then both men went back in the truck."

"Did you say anything to them?"

"No," said Robert. "I just watched."

They crossed the stream to where the bulldozer was parked, its wheels slightly off the ground, its hydraulic legs pressed down into the earth. It smelt of oil and diesel.

"What about the fox cubs?" asked Matt.

"They'll still be there," said Robert. "The vixens will probably come after dark and take them away."

"At least the bulldozer has packed up now."

They looked at the bushes it had uprooted, the soil-enclustered roots in the air, the leaves already limp. It was obvious that Weightman was intending to clear the whole wood. His men had got everything ready for the following day.

"Is there anything we can do?"

"We could immobilise the digger. We could drain the petrol."

"We could put sand in the tank."

"We could remove the carburetter."

They were fantasies, like clearing the beach of people by a mortar attack. The cab door was open, but there was no obvious way of putting the bulldozer out of action.

"What could we *really* do?"

"We've got to be here before them. They'll probably start at seven-thirty."

"We'll meet at seven."

His dad was indignant. "This was what I feared, it's the worst that could happen," he said. "If Weightman can destroy the wood, there's no limit to what he might try."

"It's a shame the National Trust didn't buy it," said his mum.

"It was a disaster."

Mr Walker made several phone calls, to local councillors and friends. Several people rang back, and the phone was in use all evening. Matthew began to feel more optimistic. When people got together, there was something they could do about it.

"We've managed to get hold of Weightman," announced his dad, late in the evening. "He's agreed to a site meeting."

The wood, the foxes, could still be safe; perhaps even the valleys and the cove.

"What time?" asked Matt as an afterthought.

"Two o'clock," said his dad.

"Two o'clock!" exclaimed Matthew. "He'll have flattened the wood by then. You'll meet him, and there'll be nothing to discuss."

"It's the best we could do," said his dad.

Matthew set his alarm for six-thirty.

They met at the hide or lookout. There was an early-morning haze lying low in the valley, its edges rising and falling about the sides of the hills. The bulldozer seemed to float in it like a yellow boat. Otherwise there was no sign of the destruction that had started, and the valley looked the same as ever. It was difficult to believe that it might be for the last time.

Conan arrived later; none of them had been able to persuade anyone else to join them. "I bet they won't start work until nine," he complained. "Nobody begins work at seven-thirty nowadays."

"Where do you think the foxes are?" asked Matthew.

"They'll have moved by now," said Robert.

They sat with their backs to the stone and watched the mist flow out of the valley, swirling down towards the sea as though a giant bath-plug had been pulled out. Suddenly the valley was clear, with the sunlight slanting low across it. It shone on the yellow bulldozer.

Robert kept his eyes on his watch. "Oh-seven-thirty hours," he intoned, on the second. All was quiet.

About two minutes later they heard a motor start high up in the next valley. They left the hide and walked down through the bracken, jumping across the stream into the field. They stood by the side of the bulldozer.

The man in the dumper truck seemed surprised to see them. He climbed into the cab.

"Are you going to bulldoze the wood?" asked Robert.

"What's it to you?"

"There's a site meeting at two o'clock."

"I haven't been told," he said.

"You can't do anything until after the meeting."

He ignored them and started the engine; the roar made further conversation impossible. The machine settled down with a lurch on its enormous tyres, as the driver retracted the supports.

The three boys went and stood in front of it, holding out their arms to cover as wide a space as possible. The bulldozer backed with a roar, and then came forward to one side of them. They moved into its path.

The driver stopped and left the cab, with the engine running.

"What are you playing at?" he asked.

"Go and ask Mr Weightman."

"Beat it," said the driver. "Get out of my way."

"He knows you aren't to start before two o'clock."

"I've had my instructions," said the man. "Do you know how much it costs to hire this digger? A hundred pounds a day! No one's going to pay that sort of money for me to sit around doing nothing."

"We're not going to move."

"We'll see about that."

He got into his cab and revved the engine. He backed further away across the field this time, and lowered the grab on the arms extended in front of it. Then he came at them fast. It was like being mown down by an enemy tank. At the last moment it slewed to one side and was past them into the thicket before they could react. There was a crash of breaking branches. Shrubs disappeared under the weight of the bulldozer, a small tree swayed wildly and went down. The machine pulled back, scooped lower, and tore out the bushes by the roots.

They could hinder it a little by getting in the way, but they could not stop it. It wasn't like television, where people stop machines by lying in front of them. There were only three of them, not enough to provide moral strength. And there were no cameras.

Robert pounded the great rubber tyres of the bulldozer in frustration as it thundered past.

By two o'clock most of the wood was flattened, except for a small patch where the two paths met. The mangled branches lay in heaps, ready for burning. The mound of the old rabbit warren, where the young foxes lay up, had been levelled. The banks of the stream had been crushed by the weight of the bulldozer. Where it was wide it had crossed by digging in its grab and using it to drag itself over. The area was now a muddy swamp, with no clear channel for the water.

People began to congregate on the footpath and survey the damage. There were Matthew's parents, Robert's parents, a few local councillors. The last to arrive was Mr Weightman, coming down over the fields in the dumper truck. He stopped opposite the group, with the stream between them. He switched off the engine and sat with one arm on the wheel; with the other hand he pushed back his cowboy hat. "What's the problem?" he asked.

Matthew's dad acted as spokesman. "We are concerned about the wood," he said. "It's part of the environment and we are very sorry to see it destroyed."

"It's mine."

"I don't deny that," said Mr Walker. "But once something has gone, it may take years to repair the damage. It may never be put right."

"I can do what I like with it."

"Not exactly, there are regulations."

"There was no preservation order on this wood."

"That's true, but —"

"Because in law it wasn't a wood. In law a tree isn't a tree unless it's eighteen inches around the trunk. None of them are that big. They aren't trees, they're just scrub."

"That may be so, but still —"

"I know the law, mate, I've gone into it."

"They may be just scrub," said Mr Walker, "but they were an important habitat for many creatures. Everything is a delicate balance. If you interfere drastically you can set off a chain reaction with unforeseen consequences."

"There were willow warblers which nested there and nowhere else," said Robert's mother.

"The nesting season's over," said Weightman. "I've kept to all the regulations."

"But where will they nest next year? And what about the stream, all the life in the stream?"

"That's all right, I'll tidy that up. I've got a digger coming to put in a new channel."

"Why do you do it?" asked Mrs James in an anguished voice. "Why do you want to change it?"

"To tidy it up," said Mr Weightman, almost in surprise. "It's just wasteland. I'm improving it, you ought to be pleased."

"It's much more than wasteland."

"To you it is, but not to everybody. You see that moor up there?" He pointed to the heather-clad hillside behind them. "I'm going to clear that too, I get a Common Market grant for doing it."

"That's madness."

"There's a food surplus already."

"Don't you care for the countryside?"

"Yes, I want to see it productive," said Mr Weightman. "But I'll tell you what I'll do. I won't clear any more of the wood, I'll leave that patch in the corner."

"Big deal," said Matthew to Robert. They left them talking, as a councillor raised the question of footpaths, and went down to the beach.

"Everyone gave in so easily," said Robert. "It was pathetic."

"He had the law on his side."

"They waited until he had done it, and then complained afterwards. They ought to have tried to stop him beforehand. What's he going to do with the beach? That'll be next."

"He'll try to make money out of it some way."

"He'll probably charge to cross the sea wall. We'll have to pay fifty pence each time we want to sit on the rocks."

They could not stop him, but they took Matt's scheme more seriously now. They were more united, more determined than before to take possession of the island and fly their flag from the peak.

"It's a gesture," said Robert. "It says that he can't do what he likes with the cove, just because he's bought it."

There was a great commotion on the beach. "What's going on?" asked Conan.

Down on the bar a group of people were clustered around a figure lying on the sand. The lifeguards were there in the centre of the activity.

"It looks as though someone has drowned."

But they would have seen the guards bringing the body out of the sea, and the bathers were carrying on as though nothing had happened. A few, leaving the water, joined the small crowd. Others came across the sand to watch. Someone ran splashing through the pool.

There was some shouting, though they could not hear the words. The crowd moved aside for other people, some carrying blankets. They caught a glimpse of one of the lifeguards kneeling over the figure. Then the bystanders closed in again.

They climbed down from the rocks and saw Print-out. He said it was a middle-aged man who had been swimming; he came out of the sea and had a heart attack. The lifeguards had tried to revive him, but they thought he was dead.

They heard a siren, and an ambulance came down to the sea wall. The ambulance men and the lifeguards carried the body on a stretcher around the side of the pool and over the pebbles. The people who had gathered around to watch gradually dispersed. Life on the beach went on as normal.

The boys went back to the rock. Matthew did not want to carry on scraping away at his initials and the date. He lay back in the sun and thought how strange it was that a man could be swimming in the sea, enjoying his holiday, and the next moment he could be dead, his life snuffed out like a candle.

"I've seen the foxes," exclaimed Robert. Each evening he had gone back to the hide to watch for them, even though he knew that the vixens might have led them a long way from their former home in the wood, that they might even have dispersed, although they were still rather young for that.

"Where were they?"

"They haven't gone far, just up the valley. I saw them last night in the top end of the field."

"They're all right?"

"Yes, I saw all five of them, the two vixens and the three cubs. There were rabbits all round them and they didn't take the least bit of notice. White-tip made a very half-hearted run at one of them that came too close, but she wasn't even trying, and it got away into the gorse. They can't be hungry."

"Has she put them in a rabbit burrow again?"

"No, the two vixens are lying up in the daytime in the old quarry."

It was just below the moorland. It had been used as a tip at one time and had a lot of builder's rubbish in it, including sheets of corrugated iron; later, earth and rubble had been added. It would be full of passages and lairs.

"I saw them first of all as they came out. They went up the valley to the cubs, in their new hiding place. . . Guess where they've put them."

"I don't know."

"They're in your adit."

"They'll be safe there," said Matthew. "Even if the Bomb falls."

"Nobody will be safe anywhere," said Robert, "if that happens."

"We've got to have a boat," said Matthew. They couldn't swim to the island, with the mast and the tools and ropes they would need to put it up. Two of them would swim, and one of them would take what they needed in a boat; it would also be there as a safety boat if the swim became too much for them.

It was no good having a sailing dinghy. The island lay to the north west of the beach and the wind often came from that direction. If it had to tack into the wind it would be separated from the swimmers, and it could take all night to get there. And sailing would keep one person so busy that he would have no time to be occupied with anything else, the swimmers and the spar.

The inflatables in the pool would be even worse. They drifted in a wind, and with one person rowing it was harder work than swimming. In an offshore wind an inflatable might never get back.

"We need something with an engine," said Matthew. What he imagined was the sort of rubber dinghy used by the Special Boat Squadron, a grey Zodiac with a Yamaha engine nosing quietly towards the rock, whilst they slipped overboard to swim the remaining distance.

"We need something like the inshore rescue boat."

"I wonder what's happening on Stennack beach," said Conan.

So for the first time that summer they went down to the village beach, on their bikes. They stood and looked at the heavy inflatable lifeboat, behind the open double doors of its garage at the top of the slipway. It was black, with a red canopy; there were white ropes to grip on to around the sides. The outboard engine was powerful enough to drive it through the surf.

It would be ideal. The whole operation could be performed easily, within an hour. They went and chatted to Mark Clark, who was on the beach. Did the surf life-saving club ever take the rescue boat out in the evening for a practice? How many went in it? Who did they have to get permission from? Could Mark Clark take it out on his own?

The answers made it clear that a minimum of three members was needed for a practice, that practices were closely supervised and timetabled, and there was no way that Mark could borrow the boat for his own use. They went back and looked at it again.

"It would make it too easy," said Matthew. There would be no skill in it, no difficulties to overcome.

"We'd better have a look at our dinghy," said Conan.

The Trembaths kept a sailing cruiser on a south coast estuary. They had a small inflatable dinghy as a tender, which they carried on the car roof and stored in the garage. The boys cycled back to Conan's house in the village and brought it out on to the drive.

It had not been used very much that summer and was soft and floppy. It was not what Matthew would have chosen. It looked too much like a toy, too much like the inflatables in the pool. It was white on top and blue underneath, and the two colours met in a wavy line. It had short oars or paddles, but there was a lightweight outboard in the garage.

They inflated it with a footpump until it was rigid, taking it in turns to pump. They ran the outboard on the bench, very briefly as it needed to be in water for the cooling system to work. It started well, on the third pull.

It would do the job, they decided. It was available, it could be carried to the beach. Meanwhile they could store it in the packing shed. Conan would take it to the island, while Robert and Matthew would swim.

It was his sixteenth birthday before the end of August, a few days before the results were due. "Would you like to have a party?" his mother asked. "You could have one here if you liked."

"No," he said.

His mum looked surprised. "Are you sure?" she asked.

"Yes, quite sure." He did not want a party before the results were out. Everyone would be thinking about the results and talking about nothing else. He would not mind a party afterwards, when at least they would know the worst. The results were on his mind all the time now, and he only escaped when planning the assault on the island.

"What would you like for your birthday then?" asked his dad.

"A wetsuit."

"I didn't think you were interested in surfing."

"I'm not, but a wetsuit would be useful."

"How much would it cost?"

"About sixty pounds new."

"Good heavens!"

"But I could get a secondhand one for much less."

His dad said he would go up to thirty pounds, if it was what he really wanted and would make good use of it.

When he was at Robert's, they looked through the local paper. There were several wetsuits advertised and Matthew rang one of the numbers. There was no reply. He rang another number. "Are you advertising a wetsuit for sale? . . . Is it still available?" Suddenly he clasped his hand over the mouthpiece. "Oh no," he said. "It's Bill Bailey." They both collapsed at the thought of buying a secondhand wetsuit from a teacher. "Yes, I'm still here," he said, uncovering the mouthpiece.

"Ask him why he's selling it," hissed Robert.

"Why are you selling it?" asked Matt. He paused and listened. "He's buying a ninety-pound suit," he whispered to Robert.

"Has it got Bailey's disease?" asked Robert.

"Has it got —?" asked Matthew, and then he pushed Robert away from the phone. "Has it got velcro fastenings?"

"He's a bit bigger than you!" said Robert.

They rode to the teacher's bungalow, to see the wetsuit. Bill Bailey answered the door. "Come in," he said, in a very matey way. "Not long now."

"No, not long," echoed Matthew. He knew at once he was referring to the exam results.

"They'll arrive at school on Thursday morning. I shall go in about nine o'clock and put up the lists behind the glass of the main entrance, so you'll be able to see them any time from then onwards. Then I'll post the individual results in the envelopes. Are you going in on Thursday, or wait for the post on Friday?"

"I'll wait till Friday," said Matt. He didn't like the idea of hunting through long lists to find his name and subjects, possibly getting it wrong in a crowd of pushing candidates. He would rather know his results by letter, all in one go and quietly on his own. Any other way was barbaric.

Mr Bailey produced the wetsuit, suspended like a guy from a hanger. It was pale blue and dark blue, with maroon patches on the knees. The bottom seemed to stick out. They laughed involuntarily because it looked so life-like, so true to the teacher's shape.

"I don't think it will fit me," said Matt.

"Try it on," said Bill Bailey. He showed him to the bathroom. "Don't forget it's inside out."

Matthew turned it right way round; it was thick and spongey to handle. It had *second skin* written across the chest in white letters. He poured talcum powder inside, very liberally — it must have been Mrs Bailey's because it was very scented. He undressed and drew the suit on to one leg, then the other. It seemed very odd to be stepping into a teacher's skin. He pulled it up and struggled to get his arms in. It took him a long time.

"Are you all right?" Mr Bailey called from outside the door.

Feeling rather foolish, Matthew walked into the hall in a haze of perfume. Robert laughed out loud.

"It's not a bad fit," said Bill Bailey.

"It's a bit wide on the shoulders," said Matt.

"You'll grow into it."

Robert fastened the neck band. "It's a bit loose in the bum," he said.

Matthew turned round like a model.

"It *is* on the large side," admitted the teacher. "But you haven't reached your full growth yet. This suit will last you for several years."

He went and looked at himself in the bathroom mirror, and then peeled the wetsuit off. He got dressed again and carried it, a dangling mannikin, back into an empty hall. Mr Bailey and Robert were in the lounge, talking about sixth form courses.

"I really wanted a black wetsuit," he said. "How much do you want for this one?"

"Thirty pounds."

"I'll give you twenty-five."

The teacher hesitated. "All right," he said.

"I haven't got the money," said Matthew. "My dad will send you a cheque."

"Don't worry," said Mr Bailey. "Bring it in next term."

"I might not be coming back to school."

"Then give it to Robert to bring in."

They parcelled it up, and went to tell Conan the story of Bill Bailey's wetsuit.

The three of them took Robert's fox-watching binoculars up to the outcrop of rocks on one side of Bluff Cove, and trained them on Penguin Island. They all knew the shape of the island well, but they wanted to have a close look at it, to see where they could land, where they could plant the mast for the flag.

Gullen was wedge-shaped, with the high cliff end facing the Atlantic. Sometimes in winter storms the sea broke right over the top. On the sheltered side it sloped away until it disappeared under the water. It was all solid rock, but it had been worn away into crevices and ledges, like the rock at their favourite spot on the beach. These ledges were like steps, and if they could land on one of them they could climb to the highest point.

There seemed to be some earth on the sheltered side, as grass clung there, and sea pinks and golden samphire. But it would not be deep enough to dig a hole in which to plant the base of a flagstaff. If the top was at all like the outcrop on which they were sitting, there would be crevices in which they could jam the mast and rocks they could lash it to.

At the end of August there would be a full moon and a spring tide. The higher the water, the easier it would be for them to land on the island. If they didn't do it this summer, they were never likely to do it again.

Matthew thought of it all the time. He imagined every stage of the expedition, trying to foresee everything that could happen and forestall any difficulties. He felt that he knew every possibility.

He walked home through the valley, going over in his mind the preparations that they had made and those still to be done. It was beginning to get dark; it seemed so early after the long evenings of early and mid summer.

The dead grass-heads on the hillsides were pale in colour, and the heather beneath them glowed.

The digger had appeared on the moorland and had started scraping the heather into piles. Several of these piles were smouldering, casting a pall of smoke over the top of the hill. There was a smell of burning in the air. The digger was parked for the night on the skyline. With its arm and grab extended to full length, it looked like a prehistoric monster slumbering in a smokey landscape.

At the top of the slope, Matthew turned to look at the scene. In summer the sun set into the sea; now it had crept back to behind the hillside. It was so near to setting that he stood and watched. It seemed to speed up as it closed with the earth; its shape became elliptical, it bit into the horizon. Very quickly it had gone. The land suddenly felt colder.

It was dark in the tunnel, with the bushes above blocking out any light in the sky. As he walked along he heard a slight noise ahead. He stopped and waited. Something was coming along the path, making a grumbling sort of noise. He could see nothing, but instinctively jumped aside as two animals, broad and low, came down the centre as though they wouldn't get out of the way for anyone. He caught a glimpse of stripes as the creatures went grunting by. They were two badgers.

He rang Robert as soon as he got home, and they went out with torches to try and see them again, but without success. Robert thought that they might have been disturbed by the digger on the moor, and were moving into the valley.

On his birthday he took his wetsuit to the beach, to try it

out. It was still unfamiliar, and Robert and Conan laughed as he struggled into it and made jokes about being in Bill Bailey's skin. Rather self-consciously he walked across the sand bar to the narrow swimming area staked out by the lifeguards with two red and yellow flags.

At first it was just as cold as swimming without a suit, but then the water between him and the skin began to feel warm, just like the shallow water on the beach after swimming further out. He would be able to stay in much longer without feeling the cold. He went back to the others, full of enthusiasm for the suit.

"It's great," he said. "You ought to try it."

"And catch Bailey's disease? No fear."

"I'm really warm, feel there."

"Ugh!" they went.

Conan in fact had a wetsuit — he had most things — though he never wore it. Robert had never tried one and they united to persuade him.

"You can wear your pants," said Matt. "You won't be in contact with Bailey's parts."

"It's too big for me."

It was true, Robert was quite a bit smaller than Matthew. "You can try it," said Matt.

Robert was tempted and put it on. He went down to the water but did not like it. He found it uncomfortable, constricting. He did not want a wetsuit, he would rather swim to the island without.

They all went down to the water's edge in their trunks for another bathe. As soon as they reached the shallows Robert and Conan turned on Matthew, grabbing him and pulling him down. With Conan holding his arms and Robert his legs, they gave him sixteen bumps — or rather splashes — in the water. Then they swung him until the next large wave approached, and flung him into it.

Whenever he went to the beach or rode his bicycle, he saw flags. There were Union Jacks still flying outside houses and shops, left from the victory celebrations after the Falklands War. In the front garden of a bungalow on the edge of the village there was a white-painted flagpole with a splendid red, white and blue flag. Matthew stopped on the opposite side of the road and eyed it speculatively. It was attached by toggles to a halyard which was cleated to the post. He had been thinking of nailing the flag to the mast, but now he saw the proper way to do it.

At the foot of the flagstaff was a sloping flower bed, planted with red, white and blue flowers in the design of the Union Jack. It was surrounded by whitewashed pebbles. A man in shirt-sleeves came out of the bungalow. Matthew, who had been thinking how easy it would be to lower the flag and detach it, shifted uneasily in his saddle and pretended that there was some problem with his brakes which needed adjusting. But the man looked very pleased. He probably thought that Matt had stopped to admire his display.

All the garages flew flags and bunting, and several hotels had the flags of tourist countries, including the Stars and Stripes, flying from poles on the front of the building or from a row at the entrance. In the town there was a Union Jack and a flag of St Piran above the council offices, and on the industrial estate the factories and businesses had banners carrying the device of the firm. One had a green and gold flag at the masthead, with the words *Queen's Award for Industry* written on it. Everywhere they flapped and strained in the breeze, bright against the blue and white sky.

But although there were so many, it was not easy to get hold of one. Neither Robert nor Conan had had any success. Matt wondered whether to buy one with the five pounds that he had saved his dad on the wetsuit. But if it was to be left on the island, it seemed rather a waste. He decided to make one.

The Union Jack would be too difficult, but the Cornish flag would be simpler. The flag of St Piran was a white cross on a black background; it represented goodness in a dark world, or — as St Piran was the patron saint of miners — the pure tin in the black ore.

He asked his mum if she had any material. She found an old blackout curtain that had been his grandma's during the Second World War. He folded it in two and started hemming the edges.

"What do you want it for?" she asked.

"To make a Cornish flag."

"Why?"

"I'd like one."

There was plenty of white material in the ragbag. He cut a cross out of an old sheet, but it was not thick enough and the black showed through. He wanted the white to shine out. He found an old tablecloth of thick material with a sheen to it. He measured and drew the cross, cut it out carefully, and then tacked it into place.

A duffel coat that he had not worn since the second year at school would provide the toggles for two of the corners. The flag would be larger than the one outside the County Hall. It would show up clearly from the land, for Weightman and all to see.

*

There was a row of flagposts outside the leisure centre, with the flags of France, Germany, Belgium and Italy, as well as the Olympic flag, the Union Jack and St Piran's Cross. Matthew took a particular interest in the Cornish flag; he decided his own rather thicker cross looked better.

They parked their bicycles in the cycle shed and queued to buy their tickets. The swimming pool was noisy, and voices echoed inside the building. The light reflected from the surface of the water in large, wobbling patterns. There was a smell of chlorine.

They changed and dived in. It was their intention to swim a hundred lengths, as they never had the chance to go any distance at the beach. They meant to do it without touching either end and without putting their feet on the bottom, but the shallow end was so crowded with children on holiday that sometimes it was necessary to put a foot down to avoid a collision. They ploughed up and down at a steady pace, keeping together and calling out the number at the end of each length. It was very monotonous, and took most of the morning.

Then Matthew thought that they ought to have a lengthy sea-swim. The next day they rode nine miles along the coast to a sheltered cove where there were no lifeguards. There was one car parked in the lane that led to the coastal path. They locked their bikes together and walked along the path on the cliff top. Then they took a narrow path through bracken that seemed to lead over the edge. From there a track went down the cliff face to a beach far below. The water looked green, with purple rocks beneath the surface. It was very still, with just a line of white along the edge where it broke gently. The sand was unmarked by feet.

They ran across the clean sand and changed on some rocks. Two fishermen stood on a promontory. A large bull seal slid through the water; his back arched and then his head broke the surface. He floated with his head high. Instead of the usual grey-black colour, he had a band of orange-brown across his face.

"It's bare flesh," said Robert. "He's had a gash, probably from the propellor of a fishing boat."

He did not seem to be bothered by it, and watched them with curiosity as they came down the beach. They waded out into the strangely still water, seeing their own limbs distorted beneath the surface.

"Why am I doing this?" asked Conan. "I'm not going to be swimming."

"You might," said Matt.

They plunged forward and swam out past the fishermen. They could no longer see the bottom and the water was much colder; there was more chop on the surface. There were several rocks in the sea, a continuation of the promontory. They made for the furthest, a low rock shaggy with seaweed which rose and fell with the swell of the water. Occasionally a wave swept over it, breaking into white foam. They rounded it, Matthew's foot touching for a moment an underwater reef, and headed for the shore. The seal came alongside; they could see that its wound was healing over.

They sat on the rocks to dry. "It's as far as Gull Island," said Conan. "Why don't we just say we've done it?"

It might have been enough for Conan, but for Matthew, and perhaps for Robert too, it was not at all the same. Only the raising of the flag on Gullen would satisfy them now.

On Thursday morning he woke up knowing that the exam results would be published that day. He had no intention of going into school to peer at the lists posted inside the glass doors, pushing and shoving to see how he had done. He had his breakfast of cornflakes and toast, looked at the paper and then took the sewing machine out of the cupboard under the stairs. He put it on the kitchen table and started to stitch his flag.

It was an old-fashioned machine with a handle to turn. He threaded the needle and started to work down one side of the cross. The bulk of the material made it difficult to handle, but he turned the corner successfully, re-adjusted all the cloth on the table, and set off down the other arm. The thread snapped. He rethreaded it and the machine began to hum once more.

The phone rang. It was Conan. He had been in to school and seen his results, had Matthew had his yet?

"No, but don't tell me," he said.

"I didn't see them," said Conan. "It's such a crush, it's all you can do to get your own."

Matt could tell from his voice that he was quite pleased. "Well, how did you do?" he asked.

He had got six subjects, two at grade B and the others grade C; he had a grade D for Chemistry.

"That's very good," said Matt.

"It's much better than I expected," said Conan. "Why don't you find out yours?"

"I'll wait until tomorrow," he said. Perhaps *his* results would be much better than he expected. The three of them had always been fairly level, ever since primary school.

He went back to the sewing machine. He stitched another arm of the cross on the flag, and then found that the thread lifted away; the machine had not made proper stitches right through the material. He took out the bobbin and put it right. The machine began to sew properly again.

Then Robert rang. "Have you seen your results?" he asked.

"No."

"I only caught sight of one of them."

"Don't tell me," shrieked Matt.

"It was nothing to worry about," said Robert. "It was quite good actually."

"How did you do?" asked Matt.

"Well . . ." Robert paused, and Matthew felt sorry for him. Obviously he had not done as well as expected. And yet he had worked the hardest of them all. "I didn't do too badly."

"What did you get?"

He spoke very apologetically. "I got six As and two Bs," he said.

"Not too badly!" exclaimed Matthew. "That's brilliant!" He felt worried now about his own results.

His dad came in for coffee, and Matt told his parents how Robert and Conan had got on. They seemed quite excited about the results.

"I can't bear the suspense any longer," said his dad. "I'm going to drive in to school. Are you coming?"

Matt did not want everyone to know except himself. "All right," he said.

The crowd had cleared by the time they turned in at the school gates, in the late morning. There were only one or two people standing by the glass-panelled doors. Mr Walker parked his car by the entrance, where all the spaces were marked with the initials of the senior staff.

With a sick feeling in his stomach, Matthew went up the steps towards the lists, like a prisoner mounting the scaffold.

It was confusing at first. The names were listed under each examination paper, so he had to find his name seven times. He looked towards the bottom of each list. He could not see that he was there at all. Then suddenly his name jumped at him.

"Physics . . . B," said his dad, getting there at the same time as himself. "That's quite good." It must have been the one that Robert had seen.

"Chemistry," said his dad. Matthew hadn't found it yet. "C . . . not bad."

But from then on it was downhill all the way. Matt saw Ds and Es, even an F. He was not sure which subjects they belonged to.

"Well," said his dad. "Do you think you can remember them?"

It did not seem to matter much whether he could or not, but he had brought with him the sheet of file paper that he had written out so hopefully, months ago it seemed, with the subject-title of all his exams and a neat box for the results. He filled them in, and when they were all written down they looked worse than he had thought. Even the Army wouldn't be interested in him. It was a disaster.

"These things happen," said his dad. "Sometimes people go to pieces in an exam, but they can usually put it right the next time."

"He's got six O levels," said his mum, determined to look on the bright side. "He's got to be given credit for that."

"Only two of them are any good," said Matthew. "The others are Ds and Es, they don't count for anything."

"But still, you passed them. It was only Art you failed."

"It was a pity you missed a C in Maths."

"Yeh." Matt felt worse about that than anything. He'd known he had not done well in some of the other papers.

"Anyway, one thing is quite clear from these results," said his dad. "There's no question really of what you ought to do. They point in one direction. You ought to go back into the sixth form and start A levels in sciences, and retake all the O levels in November."

"I want to do history," said Matt.

Or make it, he thought, seeing again in his mind's eye the ships coming home from the Falklands, the crowds cheering on the quayside.

He went down to the beach. There were as many summer visitors as ever, though only about a dozen inflatables in the pool. Once the bank holiday was over the visitors would disappear, almost overnight. The café would open if it was fine for a little while longer, and then board up its windows for the winter. The car park attendant would linger on, collecting the odd fifty pence from a few cars. The lifeguards were employed by the council until the middle of September, when their wooden hut would be unbolted from its concrete base and taken away on a lorry with the flagstaff and their notices. In its place would be put a red and white notice saying DANGER-OUS BEACH. *The lifeguard service has now finished for the season.* DO NOT BATHE AT ANY TIME.

Robert and Conan were on the rocks.

"How did you get on?" they asked, thinking his results had been in the morning post. He had not seen them again on Thursday, after going in to school.

"Dreadful," he said, putting his hands to his head and covering his face, exaggerating his reaction. "It was terrible, I only passed two subjects."

They were sorry. "What will you do?" they asked. "Will you take them again?"

"I don't know," he said.

They were clear what they were going to do, the results had more or less decided for them. There was no more talk of joining the Merchant Navy or working their way around the world. They were both going to take their A levels, Robert in sciences and Conan on the arts side.

"I'll decide later," said Matthew. "After we've been to Gullen."

"When are we going?"

"This weekend," said Matt.

It could not be left any later. The summer was rapidly passing, the schools went back the following week. It might be the last thing that they would do together, they seemed to be going their separate ways. It was now or never.

"Saturday or Sunday?"

"Tomorrow," said Matt. The moon was right, the tides were right. It gave them the rest of Friday and all day Saturday to make their final preparations.

There was a slight tension. Suddenly it was going to happen. It wasn't like getting a group together or building an underground shelter. They were really going to take the island.

"It's got to be done," said Robert. "Tomorrow evening, then."

"Okay," said Conan, rather less enthusiastically.

When they left the beach, they walked back up the valley together. The hawthorn bushes, that had been white with may-blossom at the beginning of the holiday, were now covered with red berries. There were ripe blackberries on the brambles, and a few leaves had already fallen from the trees. Those that remained had lost their freshness, burnt by the salt winds of the summer.

Where most of the wood had been was still a muddy wasteland, scarred with the caterpillar tracks of the digger. The stream flowed in a straight channel, through freshly-dug earth banks. The scraping of the surface of the moorland continued day after day, and a large area had now been laid bare. The smoke from the burning heaps of heather roots drifted over the hillside.

They scrambled down the bank to the adit and entered quietly, not wishing to disturb the foxes. They were probably far back in the hillside, beyond the roof-fall where Matthew had buried his boots, it now seemed ages ago. The cubs would just be waking up, ready to start prowling for any food they could find, shrews, beetles and snails. The vixen had stopped suckling them, though they still stayed together as a family.

Taking the same positions as before, they manoeuvred the mast out of the adit, across the stream and back up the slope to the path. Matthew examined its fittings; there was a pulley in the top through which he could pass a halyard for the flag. There was a suitable length of cord amongst the rope, which he hid in the gorse.

It was much easier carrying the spar downhill through the valley than it had been before, when they brought it up from the farm sale. They passed the despoiled wood and the junction of the two valleys where the streams and the paths both met, and continued through the lower part of the valley, exposed to the sea.

On the level path it began to seem heavy again. "It'll be awkward in the water," said Conan.

"It won't weigh as much," said Matthew. After all, physics had been his best subject.

When they were about a hundred metres from the beach, he called them to stop. There was no one on the footpaths or the hillsides. There were cars in the car park, but no one was looking in their direction. It wouldn't have mattered much if they were.

The path at this point ran alongside the stream, which was overgrown with summer vegetation, turning brown and dying back at the top but still thick with leaves at the bottom. Robert stood back, and Matthew and Conan at the two ends swung the spar. On the count of three, they let go and it crashed through the growth and splashed into the stream. The plants shook and swayed, scattering clouds of parachute seeds, and came upright. The mast was hidden in the water of the stream beneath them.

He took the heap of ropes home, and sorted them out. He put aside the terylene cord for the halyard and those ropes which would serve as stays to anchor the mast and other ropes to lash it. They also needed a towrope. Anything else that looked rotten, or was made of hemp or sisal, he threw out.

He finished strengthening the stitching of the flag, attaching the toggles. He put everything ready to take to Robert's the next morning.

When he woke up, he drew the curtain and looked outside. The trees were swaying, turning up the undersides of their leaves in the wind; many more leaves had fallen. The sky was overcast, and it looked as though it might rain. It was not very promising.

They met at the packing shed, which had become their base. They stowed the ropes and flag in the bows of the dinghy, under the flap of material that kept off the spray, and carried it down to the beach. There were very few people around. As it was Saturday, many of the holiday visitors had started their return journey, and no one was taking their place. There were about ten cars in the car park, and most of those belonged to lifeguards and surfers. The cove had an end-of-season feeling about it, with a hint of autumn in the air. Grey clouds passed low overhead, moving rapidly; the waves were high. The red flag was straining on its rope, the halyard bulging away from the pole; it was frayed and stubby after a summer's use.

They floated the dinghy in the pool. There were no other inflatables there. Overnight the high tide had taken some of the sand away from the bar, and the gap through which the stream flowed was wider. The water level had dropped.

They stood looking at the sky and the sea, for some hopeful prospect. There was none, and they looked glumly at each other. "It might improve," said Matt.

But it gave the feeling that it could only deteriorate.

Without changing, they played around in the dinghy, to make it look as though that was why they had brought it there. It would take two oarsmen, using paddles in rowlocks, and a passenger. They went round and round the pool, crossing and recrossing it as fast as they could.

They forgot about the weather.

When they left, they tied the painter to a large stone and dropped it on the bottom. They found Print-out sitting in the back of a van, and asked him to keep an eye on it for them. They bought apple pies and chocolate from the café. Then they went home, having agreed to meet at Robert's in the evening.

He packed the food, a heavy sweater and a towel in the khaki haversack that he had used for his school books and, more recently, for his beach things. He put his wetsuit into a plastic bag.

"I'm going to Robert's," he said, after the family meal.

"What are you doing?"

"We're having a sort of party. I might come home, I might stay the night."

They were not surprised. "Have you got a key?" his mum asked.

"Yes."

"Well, don't wake us up if you come in late."

There had been some showers in the afternoon, but the wind seemed to have dropped when he left the house.

They wrapped the outboard engine in a plastic fertiliser bag, having filled the tank with petrol. They had more petrol in a can. They each had a haversack full of clothing, food and flasks. The dinghy was in the pool on the beach. The mast was in the stream. They were all ready.

They could go as soon as the cove was clear. It usually emptied of people when it began to get dark. Sometimes a car with a couple of lovers would remain, the windows closed and steamed over. They would be too preoccupied to take much notice of the boys. Sometimes, especially on a Friday or Saturday evening, there would be a barbecue party on the beach. If there were, they would just have to wait until everyone had gone home.

Matthew rode down to the beach to reconnoitre. It was just getting dark, and the windows of a chalet at the top of the hill were brightly lit. Beyond it the sides of the valley were black, with the stump of an engine house showing up against the sky. There was a grey light in the west which was reflected in the sea. Matt rode slowly, braking all the way down the slope and watching carefully.

There were no fires on the beach, no lanterns glowing on the rocks. The weather had at least discouraged other people. Suddenly the headlights of a car were switched on in the car park. They shone over the stony surface and across the stream, lighting up a patch of the hillside. As the car moved off, the arc of light swept across the slope, was lost over the sea and then began to come up the road towards Matthew. He moved in to the side against the hill and waited for it to pass. The beam dazzled his eyes and then left him in blackness. Gradually he began to make out the shape of the skyline again, the hill at the end dropping into the sea, the sea itself with its white line of breakers, the island on the horizon.

He continued freewheeling down to the sea wall, still without switching on his cycle-lights. As he descended he could see the pool with the greyish blob of the dinghy swinging about within it. He came to a stop by the flagstaff; the flag was cracking as it whipped in the wind above him. Any lull had only been temporary. Beyond the wall the beach was deserted. There were no cars in the car park.

He rode in low gear up the road across the hillside, without getting off to walk. When he reached the top, he was startled by a light ahead of him, behind some fir trees at the side of the road. It was the moon, seeming enormous so close to the ground, and almost orange in colour. The clouds obscured it, but its light shone through, making them appear tattered and thin.

The other two were drinking coffee while they waited, and were reluctant to move out of the comfort of the shed.

"It's all clear," he told them.

Conan stood up with a sigh. "It's like being in the scouts again," he said.

They walked down to the beach, carrying their haversacks and the outboard engine. A squall of rain gusted across the valley, beating into their faces. Once they were in the water, thought Matt, it wouldn't make any difference to them whether it rained or not. If it had been a still, warm evening, it would have been too easy. He preferred it this way, with the wind beating the rain against them. The feeling that winter was approaching, the darkness and the cold, excited him.

They left everything behind the café, on the side sheltered from the wind and rain. Their eyes had adjusted to the darkness and there was enough light from the sky and the water and the moon for them to follow the path up the valley to the spot where the stream and footpath ran alongside each other. They felt around amongst the wet vegetation, and lifted the spar out of the water. They took it to the car park.

As they started to change behind the café wall, they heard a noise above the wind and the crashing of the waves. It was a car engine, and a moment later they saw its headlights as it turned into the car park and stopped under the sea wall. The lights went out, and then an interior light came on as the door was opened. There were two men inside, who got out and went to the boot.

The boys watched from around the corner of the building, keeping well out of sight. The spar was lying in the car park, but it was some way from the car and the men were not likely to see it unless they walked down to the stream. They were more interested in unloading the car, and for a moment Matt saw the line of a pole swing across against the sky. "They're fishermen," he said in dismay.

If they were fishing they would stay there for hours, perhaps the whole night. The expedition would have to be called off.

The door slammed, the courtesy light went out and the fishermen appeared on the sea wall, silhouetted against the sky. They stood looking at the waves, and then disappeared on to the beach. They were not carrying their fishing rods.

Another flurry of rain lashed the cove. A few minutes later they were back on the sea wall, crossing it without any delay. The car boot opened and the men seemed to be packing away again. The interior light shone briefly, the doors slammed and the engine started. The lights went on and the rear lights glowed red in the car park. The reversing light illuminated the spar, its varnished wood shining. The car went backwards, fast, almost to the mast. It stopped a short distance away, and Matt expected the men to get out and examine it. But they had not seen it behind them, and the car went forward and turned, the lights flashing briefly on the red flag. It accelerated up the slope.

"It's all ours," said Matthew, as the sound of the car died away and the cove reverted to the wind, the waves and the night.

The men must have decided that conditions weren't right for fishing, and given up. But if they weren't right for fishing, they were hardly right for anything else, and as the three boys stood, changed, on the sea wall, they wondered whether they should postpone their attempt.

Matt was all for carrying on. "If we put it off until next year, we'll never do it," he said.

"There would be no point doing it next year," said Robert. "That would be too late."

"But look at the sea," shouted Conan.

They were all watching the waves. They broke on the rocks at the side, the foam rising up almost in slow motion and crashing back into the sea to send smaller waves back across the direction of the main breakers, to meet in another explosion. Other waves smashed on the rocks and the water rushed and slid along them, swamping the boys' usual resting place and spraying the carved initials and dates. The white, broken water showed up in the faint light.

"It'll be all right once we're in it," shouted Matt. It was no worse, really, than many other times when they had bathed. A similar sea on a warm, sunny day would have been exhilarating. It was only the darkness which made it seem worse.

They could get themselves through the waves easily enough, diving through and under the breakers into the trough behind. And the spar wouldn't be too difficult, driving it ahead of them like a torpedo through the water until it was in the calmer seas beyond the waves.

It was the dinghy that was the problem. It didn't have the weight of the spar. It was likely to be turned over by the breakers, tossed about like a piece of flotsam. Once it was out beyond the waves, it too should be safe.

"We can try," said Matt. "If we can get the dinghy launched, we can go ahead. If we can't, we'll give up."

Despite the wind, it was not really cold yet, not the cold of autumn. Matthew and Conan wore wetsuits, Robert wore trunks and a tee shirt. They waded through the pool to find the dinghy, invisible at the far end. It loomed into sight and they towed and lifted it on to the sand bar, leaving it just above the waterline.

They had left their other clothes in the plastic fertiliser bag, behind the café. They took down to the boat their haversacks and the outboard motor. As there was a high risk of overturning, they made sure that everything was inside the haversacks, which they roped together, securing them in the bows with more rope tied to the support lines around the dinghy. They lashed down the paddles, and tied the baler by a cord to one of the thwarts. They brought the spar from the car park.

"The dinghy will go last," said Matthew to Conan. "We'll take the mast out beyond the waves, then we'll come back to help you."

They were ready to go, but no one made a move.

"Why am I doing this?" asked Conan, as he looked at

the impossible sea, the crests hiding the island. "I don't believe it, it's mad."

They all felt its madness, but they had come so far, there was no going back. And if they couldn't launch the dinghy, there would be a way out.

The moon had risen higher and shone now on to the waves in the cove, through a gap in the clouds. Matt took the end of the mast, and started walking into the sea.

He had swum in higher seas, though in less strange circumstances, and although it looked as though the waves would smash a person to pieces, in fact the buffeting was not severe on open sands; the danger would be if they threw him on to the rocks. Matthew turned his back to the breakers, or dived through them, or let himself be bobbed about like a cork, but all the time he was getting further out to sea and guiding the spar with him. He had felt cold at first, but the fight with the waves burned up a lot of energy, and by the time he and Robert had got the mast out into the open sea, where they could forget about it for a while he felt comfortably warm inside his suit.

"Okay?" he mouthed at Robert.

Robert made a thumbs up sign in the water.

As they swam back to shore, he could see the moon above the dark land and a track of moonlight in the troughs between the crests. Then they were in the breaking crests, and surfed on to the beach, not standing up until the water was only knee-deep.

Next they had to launch the dinghy. The outboard engine was clamped to the transom, and they carried it down to the water, lifting it over the waves until they were waist deep. They held it above their heads as a large breaker crashed into them. They were battered, but managed to stay upright.

"Now," shouted Matthew, and they surged forward, trying to gain as much ground as they could before the next large wave. It broke right over them, knocking them off their feet and snatching the dinghy from their hands. The dinghy rose upright before the wave and fell back upside down. It was carried in with the flowing water until it lost impetus and began to drift back. They towed it to the beach, drained out the water, and righted it.

"We've got to weigh it down," said Matthew. "We've got to get on to the bows when a wave comes."

They carried it out again, lifting it over the first waves until the water was too deep. Then, when a breaker came rushing down on them, Matt threw himself across the bows and the other two clung on to the sides. They were underwater and the dinghy filled, but it did not stand upright on its stern. Its buoyancy brought them to the surface beyond the crest, spluttering and throwing water out of their hair.

"Get it out," shouted Matt. The roar of the waves was loud around them.

They swam out, dragging it with them, towards the next breaker. Again they threw their weight on the bows, to hold it down when it wanted to rise on the wave. The water sloshing around inside made it slow and heavy to pull.

They survived another breaker, gradually towing it out to where the waves rolled in but were not yet ready to turn.

"Get in!" shouted Matt to Conan, who hauled himself aboard the waterlogged boat and started to bale furiously. The dinghy rose on the swell, bending its back on the peak, and Conan hung on to keep his balance. Then he baled again.

"Look out!" Robert shouted. The mast was drifting down towards them.

He and Matthew propelled it further out to sea, while Conan, kneeling in the stern of the dinghy, tried to start the outboard after its immersion. He kept pulling the cord but the engine only coughed.

"Use the paddles," called Matthew. The dinghy was drifting back towards the beach and would soon be thrown amongst the breakers again.

With a sudden roar the engine started and the dinghy moved foward with surprising speed, curving round towards the spar. They attached it to a line, and as it took the weight of the mast in the water it slowed down considerably, chugging out towards the island. Matthew and Robert followed behind.

They had got off from the beach.

It was great, thought Matthew. It was splendid, swimming steadily out to sea with the difficult departure successfully behind them. The sea rose and fell, and on the peaks he could see the island ahead of them and knew they were on course. The surface was choppy, with small wavelets that broke across their faces. The crash of the breakers was behind them.

He could feel now the current in the water, a slight tugging that pulled them up the coast. It was easy to swim across it, to head more to the west to allow for the drift. There was no undertow, no feeling of being sucked down.

He settled down to the rhythm of swimming. He swam without any sense of strain, feeling that he could continue for miles. Robert was swimming easily nearby.

There were patches of moonlight and cloud shadow on the water. He could see clearly, although he kept his head low. He could see the peak of the island all the time now, and began to distinguish individual formations of rock.

He felt tense, all his senses at the alert, as the Special Boat Squadron approached their objective. The outboard engine on the dinghy muttered steadily. Conan sat low in the stern. From time to time he baled out, and as he flung the water overboard the liquid looked solid in the moonlight.

They heard the sound of breakers again, the noise increasing as they approached the island. Gullen loomed huge above them, its base white with breaking water. Conan made for the sheltered, eastern side. He idled the engine, and Robert and Matthew swam forward and clung to the edge of the dinghy. They surveyed the island.

In the darkness, the end that sloped into the sea was a confusion of rock shapes. The water was not breaking into foam, but rose and fell ominously. At one moment it would be high on the side of Gullen, at the next it would drop away to reveal underwater rocks. It would form a pit in the sea, into which the water slid and swirled until it surged upwards into a mound again. They kept well off to avoid being sucked in.

There was no obvious place to land. They moved further around behind the island. Here the rock face was more sheer, but stepped in ledges. There was the same swell on the sea, but Matt thought that a swimmer could go in on an upsurge, land on a ledge and scramble to safety. He and Robert would land, Conan would keep the dinghy offshore ready for the return journey.

He untied the towline from the boat and, making sure there was a good length between him and the mast, fastened it around his middle. He pushed off and swam towards the island. He got as close as he dared, watching the water rise and fall. He felt the sudden tug as it surged, trying to pull him with it, and he swam back with all his force. He waited, checking that he was not entangled with the line, getting to know the rhythm of the swell.

When he knew the next surge was due, he swam powerfully forward. He was taken by it and thrown towards the ledges. The rock approached with a speed over which he had no control. He felt he would be dashed against it. Then the movement of the water slowed as it reached its peak, he grabbed for a ledge and got a knee over it. The water pulled back from him. Quickly he climbed higher, the line in his way. He passed it around a rock.

He returned to the ledge. Robert came next, riding the swell. Matthew grasped his arms and hauled him up, while the sea tried to suck him back. Robert cut his leg as he came over the ledge; he felt it and there was blood on his hands. Matt's wetsuit had protected him, though he did not yet know how damaged it had been.

They pulled in the line until the mast was below them. They used each surge of the water to lift it higher, until they could manhandle it over the ledges and up on to the spine of the island. Matthew continued up the slope to the top.

There was a sheer drop to the foam below. To the east of the island Conan was circling round and round in the dinghy, well clear of the rocks. Robert sat by the mast, head bowed, holding his leg. Matt looked across the water to the cove, seeing it from a perspective he had never seen before. It almost disappeared into a continuous cliff-line, dark and unbroken by any light. He could just make out the two hills on either side of the cove, otherwise he would hardly have known it was there. The moon rode high in the sky above it, casting a broken track across the water.

He turned from the view, and looked to see where they could plant the mast on the peak where he stood. It was very like the outcrop of granite above the cove, worn rather smoother but still with many ledges and cracks. It would hold the mast.

He called to Robert and they lifted the spar to the top. They held it upright and jammed it into a crevice in the rock. He passed a rope around the back of the rock and took several turns around it, lashing the flagstaff into position. It was solid, though not quite perpendicular. The flag was already attached to the halyard and rolled around the mast. He undid the string that held it and it broke free.

Then he pulled on the other side of the halyard, and the flag of St Piran rose slowly into the night sky. When it reached the top he tied down the halyard. The flag strained in the wind, the silvery-white cross shining in the darkness.

They had done it. Their flag flew over the island, just as the Union Jack now flew over Port Stanley. They had recaptured Gullen, just as the Task Force had recaptured the Falklands. There were no cameramen to record the moment, no crowds to cheer. But the flag was there, and tomorrow it would be seen. They had triumphed.

"Let's go," said Robert, breaking in to Matthew's moment of success.

Matt turned to him. "Are you all right?" he asked.

"No," said Robert. His leg was bleeding badly, and he was shivering with the cold.

"We'll get back to the dinghy," said Matthew. There might be a dry jumper in one of the haversacks, a hot drink in a flask, something to eat. He had imagined eating on the island, a picnic beneath the flagstaff, but they could not land the dinghy and Robert needed to return.

They climbed down to the ledge. The sea lurched towards them and receded. They would have to jump in when the water was at its height and then swim like mad to get out of the swell before it surged back and smashed them against the rock.

Matt looked at Robert. It was all right if you were fit and warm, as he was. But Robert was suffering from the cold and his leg was gashed. "Can you do it?" he asked.

"I'll have to," said Robert. He clenched his chattering teeth.

"You go first," said Matt, thinking that if Robert were swept back he would be there to help.

Conan brought the dinghy in as close as he dared.

The water rose to their feet, but Robert missed his chance. It dropped back two metres and then surged upwards. Again Robert did not jump.

"I can't do it," he said. He looked frozen and exhausted. If they got him in the water he might not have the strength to swim away from the rocks.

"Wait here," said Matt. "I'll go first."

As the water swelled up towards them, he dived as far

out as he could and swam powerfully away. Even so he could feel himself being sucked back as the water fell, and then he was clear of its pull. He hauled himself on board the dinghy.

"Robert can't make it," he said. "We'll have to take the boat in close."

They would go in on the upsurge, snatch Robert and come out on full throttle.

Cautiously, Conan brought the dinghy in closer, testing the power of the engine against the flow of water. Matthew waited for a particularly high swell, as those immediately after were more moderate. The water rose over Robert's legs, sending him back against the wall.

"On the next one," called Matthew.

The dinghy moved in, and then swept forward and sideways out of all control. They were right against the rock.

"Jump!" shouted Matt, and Robert dropped into the boat, sprawling across it as the water began to fall. The dinghy went down with it, stern first. Then as the sea came back, it righted and swept towards the rock. At the last moment it swung around, and as it did so there was an enormous crash as the outboard hit the granite.

"Get out the paddles!" shouted Matt. If the dinghy stayed where it was, they would be thrown to and fro, smashing against the rocks each time.

Conan had them ready. There was no time to put them in the rowlocks, they paddled on each side. The boat moved slowly away from Gullen.

They stopped when they were well clear, in the lee of the island. Matthew thought that the blow the dinghy had received would have torn off the transom, but it was still in place. The outboard engine had taken the full force. They had shipped a lot of water.

They pulled off Robert's soaking tee shirt and rubbed him vigorously with a damp towel. They gave him a jumper that was not too wet, and Matt bandaged his leg with the tee shirt. The flask was smashed, and the inside of the haversack was a mess. They did not want to stop to eat, all they wanted now was to get ashore.

Conan looked at the outboard, but it was damaged beyond repair, the shaft snapped. He switched off the petrol. "We'll have to row," he said.

Whilst Conan baled, Matt took the paddles and started to pull towards the dark line of the cliffs, where he knew the cove to be. After five minutes he stopped to rest. The island was still on his left-hand side, more or less where it had been when he started. He would have expected it to be well astern by now. It was further away, but they had made no progress except sideways.

"It's leaking badly," said Conan.

They changed places, Matthew baling and Conan rowing. Robert lay slumped in the bows, protected a little by the material of the cuddy. The water washed around their ankles. With constant baling it rose no higher.

When Matt took the paddles again, he checked their position. The island, with the flag flying clearly from the top, was still on his left-hand side, though if anything more towards the bows. With wind and current coming from the same direction, they were losing ground, drifting up the coast past Stennack Head.

They were on a waterlogged, leaking dinghy, drifting in

the current and unable to reach the shore, no matter how hard they rowed. One of them was suffering from exposure and a leg wound that would not stop bleeding. The whole night was before them.

"I could swim ashore," said Matthew. Once he was ashore he could fetch help for the others.

"It's too risky," said Conan. "If we can't make it in the dinghy, you couldn't swim it."

But the wind was catching the sides of the inflatable, pushing it back. Matt would be low in the water, unaffected by the wind.

"I swam across the current before."

"We've drifted up the coast, it would be more against you now."

"I think I could do it," said Matt. "And we've got to do something about Robert, we can't leave him all night."

"It's best to stick together," said Conan.

They had given up rowing as it achieved nothing, only exhausting them. They kept all their energy for baling.

The opening of the cove had long since disappeared into the line of black cliffs. The island was far away and they approached the headland, around which the current would sweep them away from the land. They kept baling and ate some of the waterlogged food, though they could not get Robert to take any. They rubbed and massaged him to try and keep him warm.

They drew level with the headland. From here they would go further and further out to sea. They would have to keep their leaking dinghy afloat throughout the night, and hope for rescue in the morning. By then it could be too late for Robert.

It seemed to Matthew that the sea beyond the headland was already rougher. They were bobbing about in the waves, which were splashing over the sides, increasing the amount of water in the bottom of the boat. He was scooping it out with his bare hands, when Conan shouted.

He looked up and saw, low down at the base of the cliffs, on the sheltered side of the headland, a single light in the whole of the dark coastline. They both shouted as loudly as they could. Matt scrambled for the torch in the haversack. He switched it on and it worked. He shone it towards the shore, waved it about, flashed it off and on.

The light on the shore moved. It swung to and fro; they could see it shining on rocks and water. It winked as a figure moved across it. He was probably a fisherman, perhaps one of the men who had come to the cove and decided it was too rough, moving to the shelter of the headland.

There was a long wait. The lantern remained on the shore, and Matt tried to imagine one of the fishermen staying there and the other climbing up the cliffs to raise the alarm. He tried to think how long it would take to get to the top of the path, to reach the car, to drive to the phone box in the village, but he lost all count of time. It began to seem too long, perhaps they had not been seen at all. The light on the shore was getting smaller as they drifted out to sea.

They were startled by a sudden explosion and a flash in the sky, falling slowly to earth behind the cliffs, followed shortly by another. The maroons had called out the lifeboat crew.

Five minutes later the headlights of a car appeared behind the cliff top, and they saw the revolving blue light of the coastguard's Land Rover. They shone their torch again, hoping it could be seen. The beam of a searchlight reached out from the cliff, feeling its way across the water. Suddenly they were in its glare, the white surface of the dinghy showing up brightly, and they turned their heads away, dazzled.

The beam held them. Then they heard above the sea the distant roar of an engine, and very soon there was the flashing red light of a helicopter in the sky. It swung in over the headland and hovered above them. The noise was intense. The downdraught of the rotorblades flattened the sea in a circle round about, and sent the dinghy swinging.

One of the crew was lowered to them. They couldn't hear what he said, but he put Robert into a harness and pointed and gestured towards the coast. Robert was winched into the helicopter, which lifted away and swung inland. As the noise decreased they could hear another engine, and saw the inshore rescue boat from Stennack Cove coming towards them at full speed. Its bows were high and it slapped the surface of the water, its outboard sending up an arc of spray which caught the moonlight. It subsided and drew alongside, and Matthew and Conan were helped aboard. With the dinghy — now almost awash — in tow, they headed back to Stennack.

The village doctor was waiting on the slipway, and a small group of people had come out of the pub. There was a burst of handclapping for the rescue team as they came up the slope. The doctor hurried them through the crowd to an ambulance, which drove them to the hospital where Robert had already been landed.

Throughout the evening Matthew had not felt afraid; he had not felt anything, too much had been happening. But after the medical checks, after the explanations to his parents, who came to the hospital in the middle of the night, after it all seemed to be over and he knew they were safe, then it began to affect him. He could not sleep, and what had seemed like an adventure turned into a nightmare. He thought of what might have happened to the three of them, afloat on a leaking dinghy in the dark, if the fishermen had not by chance gone to fish in the lee of Stennack Head. They would have drifted out to sea, and the boat would probably have sunk before morning. They might have been drowned; whether they sank or not, Robert almost certainly would not have survived the night. In the early hours of the morning, in the strange surroundings of a dimly-lit hospital ward, amongst the moans and snores of other patients, he felt the fear and guilt that he had not felt at the time.

Robert had seven stitches put in the wound on his leg, and was treated for exposure. Matthew and Conan were pronounced fit. All three of them were allowed to leave hospital the next morning, and were collected by their parents. As they came through the swing doors they were taken by surprise at the reception that awaited them. There were reporters, photographers and television cameramen.

They were bombarded with questions: why had they done it? What had they hoped to achieve? What had they felt? Had they expected to be rescued? Had they given up hope? They blinked and squinted in the pale sunlight, and muttered their replies. They were asked to pose on the hospital steps, saying goodbye to some nurses whom they had never seen before. They had their photos taken separately with their parents, in front of their cars.

The next morning Matthew opened the paper, not knowing whether he wanted to see a picture of himself or not. He scanned the pages quickly. There they were, the three of them on the hospital steps. They looked very young and scared and sheepish, much more so than he remembered feeling. He turned over without reading the caption.

They appeared again in the evening, on the local television news programme. The report began with film of Gullen; the telescopic lens zoomed in on the peak, showing the mast and the flag of St Piran flying in the breeze. Why had they done it? "We wanted to recapture the island," said Matthew. "We wanted to give it back to the people it really belongs to." But who did it belong to? Robert spoke up with some dignity, saying that the coast belonged to the people who had cared for it for generations, and that it should be preserved for them. It was threatened by the new owner, who had already destroyed a wood and part of a moor. They had no confidence in his plans for the beach, and they had raised the flag as a gesture. "It was something we had to do," said Matt. Conan looked embarrased by the whole affair.

Despite what Robert had said, the television producer had his own idea of what the story meant. There was no interview with Weightman, or anyone from the National Trust. The presenter of the programme turned from the film report to his guest in the studio, a representative of the coastguard service. "Every year we have youngsters getting into trouble around our coasts," he said. "What do you think should be done?" The expert spoke of the risks and dangers, especially of inflatables. He was in favour of more education. "It's sometimes suggested that those who are rescued should pay the cost of the operation," prompted the smooth young man in the studio. The expert said that it would not apply to juveniles. "But it's taxpayers' money," insisted the interviewer. "Why should you and I have to pay for the folly of someone else?"

They could have treated it as a story about Cornish national pride, or about the preservation of England's coastline. They had chosen to turn it into another report about young people getting into trouble.

In the television coverage of the Falklands War, thought Matthew, they hadn't only asked how much it had cost. They hadn't cut from pictures of the ships returning from the South Atlantic, the *Conqueror*, *Canberra* and *Hermes*, and complained that it was taxpayer's money that kept each ship afloat.

He went back to his room and made himself read the newspaper reports; his parents had collected others during the day. The tone was the same. A favourite word in them all was 'foolhardiness'; local boys should have been more aware of the danger. The three of them were publicly rebuked.

Why had they done it? The newspaper and television accounts forced him back to the question. Conan had never really wanted to capture the island. He had gone along with the plan because they had always done things together. It had mattered much more to Robert. The protection of the area was a principle that he was prepared to stand up for, even though, as Matt now recognised, it was not really in his character to take action. He admired him all the more for it.

But why had *he* done it? Matthew had never liked post-mortems but the aftermath of the affair, with its public criticism, concentrated his mind. He shared Robert's feelings about the landscape and the coast, and the wild creatures that inhabited it, but not to the same extent. It wasn't to protest against its destruction that he had raised the flag on the island. Nor was it to revive the tradition of the village boys, that they weren't men until they had swum around Gullen. And it wasn't just a stupid, thoughtless act, as the television had suggested. He had taken the initiative, and drawn the others into it.

He could only conclude, as he lay on his bed with the headset of his Sony Walkman over his ears, that he had been acting out a fantasy. He had thought it was real, but it was no more real than the body buried beneath the rock-fall in the adit, or their attempts to form a group. Everybody had been play-acting the whole of the summer.

He accepted the rebuke of the Press, even though it was unfair. He had known all along that it was dangerous, no 'education' would have taught him more. He had thought of everything and done all he could. It was a calculated risk. With a bit of luck, with better weather, they could have brought it off. And then it would have been a fine example of the adventurous spirit of British youth, rekindled by the Falklands War. It was all right for adults, he thought, to act out an adolescent fantasy; that was valour. But if you were an adolescent, it was 'foolhardiness'.

He was even more critical of himself than anyone else had been. There were moments when he was over-whelmed by the thought of the danger that he had led them into, and the loud beat of the music couldn't drive it from his mind. His actions had put them all at risk, Robert even more so than the others. He had brought him close to death. They had seen it approaching, it was only chance that had saved him. If he had died, how would Robert's parents have felt? How could he ever have faced them again? What could he have said that was not hypocritical and false?

His mother's face looked round the door, mouthing words. He took off the headset. A neighbour had arrived to enquire how he was, and he was expected to show himself. He switched off the tape and went downstairs. The neighbour was going on about how when she was a girl they all knew that the sea was dangerous, but nowadays everyone expected to be taken care of. If you got into trouble, someone else would rescue you.

Matthew had not been out all day, and hadn't had contact with Conan and Robert. He supposed that they had to put up with the same sort of thing. He sat and listened and looked suitably abashed.

"And what are you going to do now?" she asked, turning to him.

"I dunno," he muttered automatically. He could go on the dole like Print-out. He could fill in the application form to join the Army. . .

He glanced up and saw his mum and dad looking at him. He knew they did not really share this woman's sentiments.

"I'll go back to school," he said. "I'll take my O levels again."

He did not look forward to being back at school, especially when he learned that Robert would not be there: he had decided to go instead to the College of Further Education, where he could take a Zoology course that the school did not offer. Without Robert, he felt that all the more attention would be focused on him. He would be pointed out, the object of jokes and remarks. He thought the public telling-off would continue.

It was not nearly as bad as he had expected. He and Conan came in for quite a lot of attention, but it was mostly from the fourth and fifth year girls. The two boys had been on television, they were in the papers; it did not seem to matter that the reports were critical. They were almost heroes, and at lunchtime were surrounded by a crowd of girls. The girls weren't actually taking off their bras and waving them, but it felt a little bit like it. At the end of the day, Conan left Matthew and sat with Mark Clark's sister in the back of the bus.

One evening in September, Farmer Trevithick parked his car at the gun shoot and walked down over the side of the moor, away from the scraped earth and still smoking piles of heather at the top. He was looking for rabbits, and came cautiously down past the quarry into the field at the bottom of the valley. He walked along the side of the stream, and stopped. In the long grass ahead of him was a family of foxes. He counted five of them, and raised his gun to his shoulder. He fired both barrels in quick succession. Two foxes lay dead. The vixens survived, and a male cub who, soon afterwards, left the area to seek out new territory.

The first of the winter storms tore at the bar, carrying the sand out to sea. The waves scoured the beach, exposing bare rock. The boating and paddling pool of the

summer disappeared.

The storms that stripped the beach struck at Gullen, sending waves breaking right over the top. The mast stayed firm, anchored in the rock. The material of the flag tore and blew away, until there were only two tattered strips of fabric, straining like pennants in the wind.